# THE GOLD DISCOVERIES,

AND THEIR

## PROBABLE CONSEQUENCES.

THE

# AUSTRALIAN AND CALIFORNIAN

# GOLD DISCOVERIES,

AND THEIR

## PROBABLE CONSEQUENCES;

OR,

AN INQUIRY INTO THE LAWS WHICH DETERMINE THE VALUE
AND DISTRIBUTION OF THE PRECIOUS METALS:

WITH

HISTORICAL NOTICES OF THE EFFECTS OF THE AMERICAN MINES ON
EUROPEAN PRICES IN THE SIXTEENTH, SEVENTEENTH,
AND EIGHTEENTH CENTURIES.

In a Series of Letters.

By PATRICK JAMES STIRLING, F. R. S. E.,

GREENWOOD PRESS, PUBLISHERS
NEW YORK

Originally Published in 1853
by Oliver & Boyd

First Greenwood Reprinting, 1969

Library of Congress Catalogue Card Number 69-19683

PRINTED IN UNITED STATES OF AMERICA

# PREFACE.

THE Discoveries of Gold which have been made in California, and, more recently, in our own Australasian Colonies, are well fitted to attract attention in a commercial country like ours; and, as might have been expected, we have had no reason to complain of any lack of publications upon so important and exciting a subject. During the last four years, all sorts of works—Lectures, Manuals, Speeches, and Pamphlets, books of Travels, Notes, Sketches, Diaries, Rambles, and Revelations, in every variety of style and form—have continued to pour in upon us; some of them light and superficial enough—but many of them of great merit and ability. The history and statistics, the chemistry and geology of the subject, have been amply descanted on; but, as far as I am aware, we have not yet had any work which professes to discuss systematically its Economical bearings and probable Social results.

The following letters are designed in some measure to supply that deficiency.

With reference to the nature of the effects which are likely to be produced by the increased, and increasing, supplies of gold, many popular errors and misconceptions are abroad. To correct these being one of the objects I had in view, I have found it necessary to begin with a statement of elementary principles, and an exposition of the nature and functions of money. This I have endeavoured to do, in the introductory letters of the series, in such a way as to render the subject intelligible to those who have not previously devoted much of their attention to it, and to whom the discussions of Political Economy generally are in some measure new.

Should gold continue to be supplied to us for a few years longer, at the present unparalleled rate, it seems impossible to doubt that the consequence will be a great social and commercial revolution—a disturbance of the relations and distribution of property—not unlike what took place in England in the reign of Elizabeth. Six years ago, the annual produce of gold and silver did not much exceed twelve millions sterling—last year it was twenty-seven—now it is forty. Not a week ago, we had intelligence of the arrival of a ship

from Australia with *six tons* of gold as part of her cargo,
and of the expected arrival of another with *ten tons*.
These are startling facts, which savour more of romance
than reality—but realities they are—and thinking men
must see that such unprecedented accessions of metallic
wealth, such marvellous and astounding additions to
our existing supply of a material which forms the standard measure of commerce, with reference to which all
pecuniary contracts are adjusted, and the value of all
commodities estimated, cannot continue long, without
producing social results of a most momentous character.
Yet many men regard all this with apathy. They turn
away with repugnance from every thing which neces-
sitates thought. If we complain of the scarcity of silver,
they improve upon it, like Dr Primrose, by lament-
ing also the scarcity of gold. They have never, they
say, experienced any plethora of money—the world
will last their time—changes in the value of money,
from the discovery of more fertile mines, are always
gradual, generally imperceptible; and should the Australian and Californian gold discoveries cause a general
elevation of prices, as so many theorists and speculators
have predicted, sixty or eighty years probably must
elapse, as in the case of the increased supplies of silver

in the sixteenth century, before the effect can become apparent.

This reference to the case of the American mines—the only example of the kind which history furnishes—is so common, and at the same time so plausible, that I was induced to examine with care such records of the prices of those early days as I had access to. I found that there were two, and only two, periods at which a great and general elevation of European prices had occurred; that the first enhancement began to be sensibly felt about 1574 (nearly thirty years after the discovery of Potosi), when prices in England and over Europe rose suddenly to about three times their former amount; and that the other, which was much less marked, took place after the middle of the eighteenth century. If the reader will cast his eye over a little chart which I have constructed in a rude way, and prefixed to the present volume, he will discover no marked or peculiar increase of production at these particular epochs, to distinguish them from the remainder of the three centuries and a half over which the chart extends. Adam Smith, in his Dissertation on the "Variations in the Value of Silver," notices the fact that the American mines produced no sensible effect

upon prices in England until after 1570; but he does
not account for it farther than by remarking, that the
increase of the supply of silver would appear to have
then exceeded the demand.  Referring to Humboldt's
Essai Politique sur la Nouvelle Espagne, which furnishes us with a mass of most valuable materials, to
which of course Adam Smith had no access, I found
that what really distinguished the first of the two
periods to which I have referred, was a great reduction
of the cost of producing silver, caused by the introduction of the process of amalgamation, and the discovery,
about the same time, of the great quicksilver mine
of Huancavelica in Peru; and that what distinguished
the second period was a still further reduction of the
price, and enlargement of the supply, of the same
material, which is so essential to the success of silver
mining.   Having thus got hold of the thread, I had no
difficulty in finding my way through the labyrinth.   I
have stated the argument as clearly and succinctly as
I could in my *tenth* letter; and in the seven following
letters, I have adduced in detail the historical evidence
upon which I rest my conclusion—that the American
mines did not produce their effect upon European prices
for eighty years after the discovery, simply *because* eighty

years elapsed before any material reduction took place in the cost of producing the metal which then formed the standard of money in every country of Europe.

In the succeeding letters, my object has been to show that gold is produced under different conditions from silver, and that we have not now to wait, as our ancestors had, for the discovery of more abundant mines of quicksilver, the introduction of new chemical and metallurgical processes, and the application of extensive capital to mining operations; in short, that the case of the American silver mines is not analogous to that of the Australian and Californian gold-fields; and that whether we look at the present unprecedented importations as likely to produce an enhancement of prices by the agency of increased supply, or of diminished cost, we shall grossly deceive ourselves if we expect that the effect of the recent discoveries will be as tardy as that of the importations of silver in the days of the Tudors.

The next subject which claims our attention is the relative value of gold and silver, and the laws which regulate the distribution of the precious metals among the different countries of the world. In the three succeeding letters, " On the Principle of International Values," I have endeavoured to demonstrate that the higher or lower range of prices in each individual country depends on the relative efficiency of its labour (a principle first pointed out by Mr Senior), and to explain the manner in which cost of production operates on the value of the precious metals as imported commodities. These letters (22d, 23d, and 24th), I may add, are intended more for the scientific than the popular reader, and may be passed over by those who have not been accustomed to the abstract discussions of political economy.

In the concluding letters, I have endeavoured to point out the nature (though, of course, *not* the extent) of the effects which the gold discoveries are likely to produce on agriculture, commerce, and manufactures, and on the material prosperity of the different classes of the community.

The more recent accounts from Australia, which arrived as the sheets were passing through the press, I have been obliged, as I best could, to throw into notes, which sometimes bear an undue proportion to the text; but for such imperfections I must throw myself upon the indulgence of the reader. The letters were written not consecutively, but in detached portions, at such uncertain intervals of leisure as I could command during the last autumn. They will be found, I fear, to bear the marks of haste, and of the many disadvantages under which they were composed; but I was averse to delay the publication, because I conscientiously believe, that the facts which are stated, and the inferences fairly deducible from them, if carefully studied, will tend to the dissemination of sounder opinions than are now generally entertained upon a subject which I cannot but regard as of intense interest, as well as of great practical importance, to all ranks and classes of society.

November, 1852.

# CONTENTS.

## LETTER XXI.

## LETTER XXII.

## LETTER XXIII.

## LETTER XXIV.

## LETTER XXV.

## LETTER XXVI.

## ERRATA.

Page 18, note, *for* lib. *read* liv.
— 21, note, *for* lib. *read* liv.
— 44, note, *for* 24th June *read* 25th June.
— 122, line 12, *for* 1663 *read* 1563.
— 134, line 4, *for* 8th Elizabeth *read* 15th Elizabeth.

# LETTER I.

*Introductory—Origin and use of money.*

As you seemed to think that the considerations which I threw out lately upon the subject of money, and of the laws which determine the value and distribution of the precious metals,—and more especially the view which I then ventured to take of the Effects likely to be produced on the permanent value of the standard, by the unprecedented streams of metallic wealth which are now pouring in upon us from the Gold-fields of Russia, California, and Australia,—were worthy of a more deliberate and accurate treatment than it is possible to bestow upon such subjects in conversation, I now proceed, in fulfilment of the promise which I gave you, to examine and discuss these abstruse matters at length in a series of letters.

The whole subject being in some measure new to

you, it is essential, in order to give you a sound and comprehensive knowledge of it, that I should begin at the foundation, with a statement of first principles. Not that I would have you to believe that this subject is at all so complex and difficult as is generally imagined. There are branches of the science of Political Economy far more complicated and unmanageable than that which treats of the nature and functions of money. It may cost you some pains, indeed, to obtain a thorough comprehension of the subject of Exchange;* but even as regards that technical and forbidding subject, much —I might almost say every thing—depends upon your making yourself thoroughly master at the outset of a few elementary principles. When this has been accomplished, and the rudiments have become familiar, you will find that your task is already half accomplished, and your future progress rendered easy and secure.

Writers upon this subject have generally been misled by an undue love of system. They are prone to go back to a fancied primitive state of society, of which history affords us no trace, and which probably never

* For a full exposition of the theory of Exchange, see *Philosophy of Trade*, book v.

existed anywhere, except in their own imaginations. If we could suppose a time when men were as savage as the monkeys of Buffon, when each man, without the aid of his fellows, supplied himself with the few necessaries which are absolutely essential to the sustentation of animal life, living upon roots or cocoa-nuts, sleeping under trees, and clothed with leaves or skins, —in such a condition of human life there would be little or no necessity for interchanges of any kind, and we might suppose the simple traffic of a race of men so rude, and of a period so remote, to be carried on by direct *barter*.

No doubt all commerce does ultimately and in effect resolve itself into barter; but the inconveniences attending the direct exchange of one commodity for another must have manifested themselves so early and so obviously, that it is difficult to conceive even the common and limited domestic traffic of the most barbarous tribes to have been carried on without some common measure of value and medium of exchange,—without, in short, the intervention of some commodity calculated to perform, with greater or less accuracy, the functions of *money*.

Value is relative. It is impossible even to express

the value of one commodity without making reference to some other commodity in which that value is estimated. If a yard of broadcloth exchange for two ounces of silver, we say that the value of 100 yards of cloth, estimated in silver, is 200 ounces, and the value of 100 ounces of silver, estimated in cloth, is fifty yards. This is sufficiently obvious. It is not quite so obvious perhaps, but it is equally true, that without some *third* commodity, some third subject of exchange,—be it labour, be it gold, corn, or what it will,—we should have no measure, no rule, whereby we could correctly determine how much of the one commodity should be given in exchange for a specified quantity of the other,—in other words, how much of the one can be exchanged for a determinate portion of the other without loss or gain. If, at the same time and place, a yard of broadcloth and two ounces of silver are respectively the products of four days' labour, then we say that fifty yards of cloth and 100 ounces of silver are of equal value, or, according to another phraseology, that their value is at par. The *third* commodity (labour) thus chosen as a measure of value, may be more or less fitted accurately to perform the function to which it is applied. Into that I do not at present enter. All

I contend for here is, that without some third commodity, or subject of exchange, we should have no measure of value at all. I shall have occasion to revert to this when we come to the intricate subject of international values.

Labour, it is true, might be universally adopted as a measure of value. But, as Adam Smith remarks, " The greater part of people understand better what is meant by a quantity of a particular commodity than by a quantity of labour. The one is a plain, palpable object; the other an abstract notion."* Hence, for the purposes of commerce and everyday life, some tangible commodity, the product of labour rather than labour itself, is fixed upon as a measure wherewith to compare the rising and falling value of other commodities.

A measure of value, however, is not more wanted than a *medium of exchange*. Even if we knew what quantity of one commodity should be given for a determinate portion of another, no exchange in most cases could take place. " The butcher has more meat in his shop than he can consume, and the brewer and the baker would each of them be willing to purchase a part

* Wealth of Nations, book i. chap. v.

of it. But they have nothing to offer in exchange except the different productions of their respective trades, and the butcher is already provided with all the bread and beer which he has immediate occasion for. He cannot be their merchant, nor they his customers."* As civilisation advances and labour is more divided, this inconvenience increases, and at length becomes intolerable. " What difficulty must ensue," says Mons. Say,† " were every one obliged to exchange his own products specifically for those he may want; and were the whole of this process carried on by a barter in kind. The hungry cutler must offer the baker his knives for bread; perhaps the baker has knives enough, but wants a coat; he is willing to purchase one of the tailor with his bread, but the tailor wants not bread but butchers'-meat; and so on to infinity. By way of getting over this difficulty, the cutler, finding he cannot persuade the baker to take an article he does not want, will use his best endeavours to have a commodity to offer which the baker will be able readily to exchange again for whatever he may happen to need. If there exist in the society any specific commodity, that is in request, not merely on account of

* Wealth of Nations, book i. chap. iv.
† Traité d'Economie Politique, 4me edit. lib. i. chap. xxi.

its inherent utility, but likewise on account of the readiness with which it is received in exchange for the necessary items of consumption, and the facility of proportionate subdivision, that commodity is precisely what the cutler will try to barter his knives for; because he has learned from experience that its possession will procure him without difficulty, by a second act of exchange, bread or any other article he may wish to obtain.

" Now *money* is that commodity."

# LETTER II.

*Functions of money—various materials which have been employed to perform these functions.*

In my last letter I endeavoured to explain the necessity which exists for fixing on some commodity in universal request as a medium of exchange, and I trust that you will keep in view, as a cardinal fundamental principle, never for a moment to be lost sight of throughout the discussion upon which we are about to enter, that money discharges two distinct offices.

(1.) It is a common measure of value.

(2.) It is a universal instrument of exchange.

The commodity which alone can perform these functions accurately must possess intrinsic value,—in other words, must be a universal *equivalent*, the product of labour and capital, like the other commodities whose value it is to measure, and whose exchange it is to facilitate. But this I shall demonstrate more at length in the sequel.

Among different nations, and at different times, various commodities have been employed as money— the thing made choice of for this purpose being always that most highly esteemed and most generally in request.

Mungo Park tells us, that when the Europeans first began to traffic with the natives on the river Gambia, the commodity most in request among these barbarians was *iron*. A bar of iron, in consequence, became the measure of value, or the money-unit; but being too unwieldy to serve as a medium of exchange, it soon became a mere nominal standard. A *bar of rum*, consisting of four or five pints, was given in exchange for a *bar of tobacco*, consisting of twenty or thirty leaves.*

In the same way, I have been told that the natives of the northern parts of Canada, in their intercourse with Europeans, adopt a *beaver* as their standard. The fur of the beaver having originally been most generally sought for, a beaver has become the standard of com-

* Traité d'Economie Politique, par J. B. Say; lib. i. chap. xxi.

parison, and all other commodities are estimated as worth so many beavers. In Abyssinia, *salt* was made use of as money. At Newfoundland, *dried cod* formerly performed the same office; and in some parts of India and Africa, a certain description of *shells:* In other countries, *hides* or *dressed leather.* Adam Smith relates, that in his day there was a village in Scotland where it was not uncommon for a workman to carry *nails* instead of money to the alehouse or baker's shop;* and I have heard of another village in the Highlands of Scotland where *eggs* are employed as money in the purchase of tea, sugar, or tobacco.

*Cattle,* although obviously the worst fitted for a circulating medium, were used in ancient times as a measure of value and instrument of exchange. Homer tells us that the armour of Diomede cost nine oxen, that of Glaucus a hundred. " A warrior," says Mons. Say, " that wished to arm himself at half the price which Diomede's armour cost must have been puzzled to pay four oxen and a half."

The objection to the employment of such articles as I have enumerated as mediums of exchange is obvious

* Wealth of Nations, book i. chap. iv.

enough. Most of them are perishable; and such of them as are readily divisible into proportionate parts are not sufficiently portable to be readily transferred from hand to hand.

Another circumstance renders them still less fitted to serve as a standard for comparing the value of other commodities,—their own value is as uncertain and fluctuating as that of the things to be compared. No commodity, indeed, is entirely free from this objection;—the metals are perhaps more so than others; yet had iron, for instance, been selected with us as the material of money, as it was in Sparta, how great a change must recent years have witnessed in the money-prices of all things. The quantity of that metal which is now produced and brought to market in the United Kingdom is more than ten times greater than it was at the beginning of the present century, while the cost of its production is probably less by two-thirds. Lycurgus directed iron to be used as the material of money, in order to increase the difficulty of hoarding it, or of transferring it in large sums. What would be thought at the present day of employing as a circulating medium a material of which this island alone produces annually two and a half million of tons!

In former days, when a ton of iron was worth three ounces of gold, or forty-five ounces of silver, had any one engaged to deliver to his creditor one ton of iron yearly in payment of a debt, he would now be paying his debt by delivering a commodity worth probably little more than one-fifth or one-sixth of the former quantities of the precious metals. As well might we employ a material which contracts and expands with every change of temperature as a measure of length or distance, as a commodity which thus fluctuates in its own value as a standard for comparing the values of other subjects of exchange.

Hence all civilized nations, ancient and modern, have by common consent, as it were, adopted the precious metals, or *gold and silver*, as the fittest and most accurate measure of the value of other commodities, and the best medium for effecting exchanges. The reasons which have induced them to select these metals in preference to all other commodities, I shall examine in my next letter.

# LETTER III.

*Reasons why the precious metals have been selected as the materials of money.*

AMONG other properties which adapt gold and silver more than other commodities for being employed as the materials of money, I shall enumerate only the *six* following, viz. :—

1. Their greater *uniformity of value.* The value of the precious metals is not absolutely uniform, but it has hitherto been more so than that of any other commodities with which we are acquainted. As we shall afterwards see, within a century after the discovery of America, the value of silver in relation to commodities was nearly as much reduced by the more abundant mines which were then laid open to European industry, and the introduction of amalgamation and other metallurgical processes, as the price of iron has been in

the present century by the improved method of smelting, and the introduction of the hot blast.  But such
changes in the value of the precious metals as were
then witnessed, and as we seem now destined, after the
lapse of three centuries, to witness again, are of comparatively rare occurrence ; and the greater uniformity
of value which characterizes the precious metals still
eminently fits them to be used as the materials of
money.

2. Their *uniformity in quality*.  No other commodities are so perfectly homogeneous as gold and silver.
Iron, for example, varies in quality, and notwithstanding the enormous quantity of that metal which is produced in this country, we still continue to import iron
of a superior kind from Sweden for conversion into
steel and the manufacture of cutlery.  The physical
qualities of pure gold and fine silver, on the contrary,
are at all times, and in all places, exactly the same
wherever found, whether washed from the sands of
Africa or Brazil, or dug from the mines of Mexico, or
obtained from the more recently discovered deposits of
California and Australia.  The relative weight, therefore, of a specific portion of either metal, in its pure state,
at once determines both its quantity and its value in re-

lation to every other portion of the same metal; and this quality fits it for being employed as a measure of value.

3. Their *divisibility*. This also is a primary requisite in a measure of value. Gold in malleability and ductility exceeds all other metals. It may be beaten into leaves $\frac{1}{282,000}$th of an inch in thickness, and a single grain may be drawn into 500 feet of wire, while an ounce of gold upon silver may be extended to more than 1300 miles in length. Silver is scarcely less ductile. It may be extended into leaves $\frac{1}{10,000}$th of an inch in thickness, and drawn into a wire finer than a human hair. A single grain may be extended 400 feet. The precious metals being thus divisible into minute portions, and capable of being united again without any sensible loss, are well fitted for the purposes of money, as the quantity of the metal can be so exactly apportioned to the value of the commodities to be exchanged.

5. Their *portableness*. They unite great value with small bulk, and are thus better suited than iron, copper, or other metals for being employed as a medium of exchange. So heavy, we are told, was the iron money of Sparta that a cart and two oxen were necessary to carry home ten minas,—a sum equal to about £20 of our money.

6. The last distinguishing quality of the precious metals to which I shall advert at present is their *not being easily counterfeited.* Their capability of receiving and retaining impressions enables the issuer of money to affix to determinate portions of these metals a stamp, which is a public voucher of their weight and fineness; while their specific gravity, which differs from that of other metals, facilitates the detection of counterfeits.

Such are some of the properties which peculiarly adapt the precious metals for the purposes of a circulating medium, and which have induced polite and commercial nations to select them as the materials of money, the instrument for effecting exchanges, and the common measure of property. To fit them for the performance of these functions, it becomes necessary to divide them into larger and smaller portions of ascertained purity, bearing a known proportion to each other. Hence the origin of *coins,* of which I propose briefly to treat in my next letter.

# LETTER IV.

*Rules to be observed in the coinage and issuing of money.*

COINS are simply portions of one or other of the precious metals, the weight and fineness of which, for the purposes of commerce, are vouched and guaranteed by a stamp affixed to them by the sovereign power of the state.

To enable them to resist friction, it becomes necessary to mix them with copper, or some other metal which is less valuable, although harder and more tenacious than gold or silver; but in estimating the value of coins, the inferior metal is never taken into account. Even when gold coins are alloyed with silver, the value of the alloy is considered not more than equal to the expense of separation. The denomination of coins, therefore, in all cases indicates simply the weight and fineness of the metal of which each is mainly composed.

The weight is, of course, more easily ascertained than the purity, assaying being a complex and difficult process, requiring previous experience and some acquaintance with chemistry.

In ancient times, coins passed by weight, and not by tale. Abraham weighed to Ephron the 400 shekels of silver which he gave for the field of Machpelah, and they are called " current money with the merchant." When David purchased the thrashing-floor of Ornan the Jebusite, he gave to Ornan " six hundred shekels of gold by weight." Even in our own country, and in much later times, coins did not pass simply by tale; for we are told that the revenues of William the Conqueror were received at the exchequer by weight.*

The denomination of coins has now ceased to express, as it did originally, the quantity of metal contained in them; and hence a certain degree of mystery has gathered round a subject which is in its own nature sufficiently clear.

If you ask me the question which has been so often put of late, " What is a pound?" I can give you no better answer than in the words of Sir Robert Peel:—

* Wealth of Nations, book i. chap. iv.

"*I cannot*," said he, "*by any effort of my understanding form any other idea of a pound-sterling, but a certain determinate weight of gold or silver.*" Had any one in the reign of William the Conqueror put the same question, his ignorance would have justly exposed him to ridicule. The pound-sterling, then, and for 234 years afterwards (down to the 28th of Edward I.), contained a Tower pound of silver, of the same fineness as our present money. The penny consisted of a real pennyweight of silver, or the 240th part of a pound. Even the shilling was indicative of a certain weight of the metal, as may be discovered from an old statute of Henry III. Had any one in those days asked the modern question, "What is a pound?" or "What is a penny?" he would have been answered at once—A pound is a pound weight of standard silver, a penny is a pennyweight of standard silver. Any one possessed of a pound weight of the metal, by carrying it to the mint, could have had it at once converted into a pound-sterling. Any one possessed of a pound-sterling, who wished to use the metal contained in it for the fabrication of plate or of ornaments, had only to throw it into a melting pot.

Nor is the case in reality different at the present day. Names, not things, have changed, and gold has become the standard in place of silver, but the principle is precisely the same. The same question must still receive the same answer—a pound-sterling is nothing else than a certain determinate weight of gold, of ascertained purity.

It seems of little importance whether gold or silver be selected as the standard of money, but one of them can alone form a standard. "Two metals, as gold and silver," says Locke, "cannot be the measure of commerce botn together in any country, because the measure of commerce must be perpetually the same, invariable, and keeping the same proportion in all its parts; but so only one metal does or can do, to itself; so silver is to silver, and gold to gold; but gold and silver change their value one to another, for supposing them to be in value as sixteen to one now, perhaps the next month they may be as fifteen and three quarters, or fifteen and seven-eighths to one. And one may as well make a measure, namely a yard, whose parts lengthen and shrink, as a measure of trade of materials that have not always a settled invariable value to one another."*

The weight and fineness of the coins of a country

---

* Locke's Works, vol. ii. p. 72, folio edit. 1722.

are matters of arbitrary arrangement. The sovereign power orders a pound, an ounce, or any other determinate quantity of the metal, of a given fineness, to be coined into a certain number of pieces. Each has a peculiar stamp affixed to it, which guarantees its weight and purity. But this is all that is effected by coinage. It is of no importance what the legal weight and fineness are, so that they be fixed and known; "but *once settled*, it is the interest of every country that the standard of its money should be inviolably and immutably kept to perpetuity; for whenever that is altered, upon what pretence soever, the public will lose by it."*

As I have elsewhere remarked,† a just theory of money requires us to consider coins simply as portions of the material of which they are composed, and they are so in fact when issued under the six following conditions, viz. :—

1. The metal selected for coinage must be homogeneous, uniform in quality, and capable of being converted from bullion into coin, and from coin into bullion again, without loss either in weight or fineness.

* Locke's Works, vol. ii. p. 49.
† Philosophy of Trade, p. 132.

2. The mint must be open to every one who may choose to carry bullion thither for coinage.

3. The bullion when carried to the mint must be converted into coin instantly and gratuitously, without delay or loss of interest, and without seignorage or deduction of any kind.

4. One metal must form the only material of money, the sole basis of the currency, or subsidiary coins of other metals, if allowed (as is the case with our silver and copper coins), must be so regulated that the metal forming the standard shall not come to be valued in such subsidiary coins, or be driven out of circulation by them, or by paper money not instantly convertible into the standard metallic money, at the option of the holder.

5. The coin in circulation must be kept constantly up to its full legal standard in weight and fineness; and,

6. There must be perfect freedom of trade in the precious metals—perfect liberty to export and import coin and bullion.

When these conditions are observed, coins may be considered as nothing else than portions of the metal of which they are composed; and it will be the business of my next letter to prove to you, that although the

*value* of the precious metals may rise and fall in relation to commodities, the *price* of the metal forming
the standard (as gold is in this country), that is, its
value estimated, not in commodities, but in the current
coin of the realm, never can change, and that the sum
of £3, 17s. 10½d. is in reality only *another name* for
an ounce of gold of our present standard, in the same
way as a pound-sterling was another name for a Tower
pound of silver in the days of William the Conqueror.

# LETTER V.

*Market and mint price of gold and silver.*

YOU seem to think that the doctrine announced at the end of my last letter, namely, that the price of the metal forming the standard of money can neither rise nor fall, as long as all the conditions I have specified are observed, if it be not positively heterodox, has at least a very paradoxical air; and you ask me to explain why if this be so the price of gold in Australia should fluctuate so much,—rising in some instances to £4, and in others falling to £2, 18s. per ounce. I cannot blame your scepticism when I find an author of such high and deserved reputation on monetary questions as Mr Thornton asserting, " that bullion is a commodity and nothing but a commodity; that it rises and falls on the same principle as all other commodities; that it becomes, like them, dear in proportion as the circulating medium for which it is exchanged is rendered cheap, and cheap in proportion as the circulating medium is rendered dear;"* and Mr Blake, so much and so justly extolled by Mr Huskisson as a writer upon exchange, maintaining, "that bullion must be subject to the same variation in its price from an alteration in the value of currency as any other commodity," and "that if the value of currency is diminished, the prices of all commodities must advance, and bullion among the rest;"† and Sir Archibald Alison, who has paid so much attention to the subject, formally asserting, that "the difference between the mint and market price of gold only shows the difference in value of that precious metal *at the time the mint price was fixed and the present moment*,"—and writing a work to persuade us that the Bank of England should be authorized to pay their notes in gold or silver, *at the market and not at the mint price of these metals*.‡ A few sentences, I hope, will make this matter quite plain to you.

Our mint regulations order a troy pound of standard

* Thornton on Paper Credit, p. 202.

† Blake's Observations on the Course of Exchange, pp. 51, 52.

‡ England in 1815 and 1845, or a Sufficient and a Contracted Currency; pp. 56, 93.

gold (gold eleven parts fine) to be coined or cut into
$46\frac{2}{40}$ pieces, called sovereigns or pounds-sterling. It
follows necessarily that an ounce of the same metal, or
a twelfth-part of a troy pound, will, when the conditions
mentioned in my last letter are observed, sell or exchange for a twelfth-part of $46\frac{2}{40}$ sovereigns (£46, 14s.
6d.), or $3\frac{14}{180}$ sovereigns (£3, 17s. 10½d.)   With us the
*third* and *fifth* conditions are not strictly observed
(although perhaps they are both observed as strictly
as the nature of the thing admits of in practice), and
consequently the market price of gold bullion, even before the recent statute requiring the Bank of England
to receive standard gold at the fixed price of £3, 17s. 9d.,
was generally somewhat below the mint price,—most
frequently £3, 17s. 6d., instead of £3, 17s. 10½d.   Examine the lists of prices for 100 years, and you will
find that the divergence of the market from the mint
price of gold has never much exceeded this, if we except
the twenty-three years of the bank restriction, when we
had positively no standard, and the period which preceded the reformation of the gold coin in the early part
of George the Third's reign.   The statute to which I
have just referred practically facilitates the conversion
of bullion into money; but the mint price is fixed in-

dependently altogether of the operation of that statute. The mint by law is open to every one—to private individuals, as well as to the Bank of England. The bank, in exchanging its notes for standard gold bullion at the rate of £3, 17s. 9d. an ounce, comes in place of the individual, and does nothing more in reality than give an acknowledgment for so much metal, and an undertaking to deliver it again to the holder in the shape of coined money at the rate of £3, 17s. 10½d. an ounce. The difference of 1½d. probably does not exceed the interest which the party would have lost by the delay, had he carried his bullion to the mint instead of to the bank.

You will now begin to see why the market price of gold in Australia may be above or below the mint price. It has not been assayed—its purity has not been ascertained. Some portions of it are purer than the British standard of twenty-two carats (or eleven parts) fine, and may sell for more than £3, 17s. 10½d.; while other portions are below that standard, and will consequently sell for less. Unfortunately no mint has been yet established in Australia,* and the metal consequently

---

* A proposal having been made to have a branch of the Royal Mint established at Sydney, Earl Grey, then Colonial Secretary,

must be sent to London for coinage.    The transmission
of gold is attended with considerable risk and delay.

in a despatch to the Governor-general, Sir C. A. Fitzroy, dated
20th February 1852, thus states the reasons which induced him
to regard the measure " as of very doubtful expediency :"—" In
considering the question, whether it is desirable to establish a
Colonial Mint, you will bear in mind that it would be unsafe to
infer from the apparent want of a ready mode of converting gold
into coin, which was experienced during the first few months
after the discovery of gold in the colony, that the same want
would continue.    The value of the gold thrown into the market
in a short time when this unexpected discovery took place, was
so large in proportion to the capital available for its purchase,
and to the amount of coin then in the colony, that a great fall
in the price of gold dust, and of uncoined gold generally, was to
be expected in the first instance.    Accordingly it appears that
gold has been sold in the colony at 60s. an ounce, and even, I
believe, in some cases, at a lower price, though its intrinsic value
is known to be 77s. 10d.    But the profit derived from the purchase of gold at so low a rate cannot fail to attract capital from
other quarters, and especially from this country, into the business,
and the deficiency of coin to carry on the increased transactions
arising from the discovery of gold is certain to be in like manner
supplied by those who will find it advantageous to make remittances in this form ; accordingly I am informed that a large
amount of capital and considerable remittances of specie have
already been sent to the colony, and this process will certainly
continue so long as high profits can be made by it, and it is thus
shown to be required.    Hence I entertain no doubt that in a

Freight, interest, and the expense of insurance, therefore are to be deducted from the price ; or a high premium must be paid to the banker or bill-seller who encounters the risk and bears the expense of transit. The price of gold in London is one thing—the price in Australia of a bill of exchange, which is a warrant for the payment of a determinate quantity of gold in London, is another and a very different thing.

Were a mint established at Sydney or Melbourne for the instant and gratuitous conversion of gold bullion into sovereigns, the price of the metal would no longer

very short time the price of uncoined gold will rise, and will approach so near to the value the metal would bear when coined as merely to leave the usual rate of mercantile profit on the transmission of gold to this country to be converted into coin ; but whether the gold is remitted to this country for the purpose of being coined, or is coined on the spot, the expense will directly or indirectly fall upon the colony, and more particularly on those by whom the gold is found," &c. &c.

This reasoning proceeds upon the assumption that the low price of gold in the colony, at the period referred to, was caused by a scarcity of sovereigns wherewith to purchase it ; whereas the true cause was, and is, the want of an authoritative assay to ascertain and vouch its quality. No exportation of coined gold from this country, however great, will supply that want. In the meantime, the colonists are confessedly selling for 60s. or 64s. a commodity intrinsically worth 77s. 10d. an ounce.

fluctuate in Australia as it now does—it would not fluctuate at all ; although the transmission of money to
this country would still of course be attended with expense.   It is not the comparative abundance of bullion
and scarcity of coin in the Australian market which
depresses the market below the mint price.   The price
is kept down by the doubts which the purchaser enter-
tains of the purity of the metal in the absence of an
assay, and the impossibility of converting it into money
without sending it to London.

Where a mint is established, and the proper regulations are observed, when the coin is perfect according to
the standard fixed upon, whatever it be, and the melting and exportation of it freely permitted, the market
price of bullion cannot deviate from the mint price by
reason of an enlargement or contraction of the supply
from the mines.   To repeat what I have said in another
place,* the best mode of testing the effect of mere limi-
tation or enlargement on the price of the metal forming
the standard is to suppose the present circulation to be
doubled in numerical amount, and at the same time
each coin, in consequence of the more abundant supply

---

* Philosophy of Trade, p. 344.

of the metal, to be doubled in weight. In that case the price of bullion, on the principles of those who think that the price of bullion is raised or depressed by the enlargement or contraction of the currency, must *rise* to £7, 15s. 9d. per ounce, or *twice* £3, 17s. 10½d. On the contrary, it is obvious that it will *fall to one-half* of £3, 17s. 10½d., or £1, 18s. 11¼d. per ounce. The case is this : I am possessed of two ounces of standard gold, of gold twenty-two carats or eleven parts fine. I carry that quantity of bullion to the mint, and I receive of the new money £3, 17s. 10½d., or £1, 18s. 11¼d., for *each* of the *two ounces*. On the other hand, why should any one give me *more* than £1, 18s. 11¼d. for an ounce of standard gold, when he can at once obtain that quantity by putting £1, 18s. 11¼d. of the (supposed new) current coin into a melting pot? The numerical amount of the circulation makes no difference either to the buyer or seller of gold bullion, which, by supposition, is the sole material of which the circulating medium is composed. The sum of £3, 17s. 10½d. is not, as certain writers appear to suppose, an antiquated assize value put upon gold by kings and parliaments at some bygone period of our history. It simply marks a *relation of quantity*, which is eternal—it is *another name* for an ounce of gold—it *is* an ounce of gold; and while the present mint regulations are observed, be the supply from the mines what it will, must be the price of an ounce of gold, and cannot cease to be so, anymore than a *foot*, ordered to be divided into twelve equal parts, can cease to be equal to *twelve inches.*

I cannot express this better, or make the subject clearer, than by quoting the language of an able writer in the Times newspaper:*—" Some people are still found to ask whether the bank is to go on giving the price of £3, 17s. 9d. per ounce for gold; whereas all that the bank gives when it issues a note is an acknowledgment that a certain amount of gold has been deposited with it, which the bearer may have back whenever he likes to apply for it. *Gold constitutes the general measure of price, and is therefore the only thing which has not a price of its own.* It is simply receivable at the rate mentioned; that is to say, when one man talks of owing another £3, 17s. 9d., he means that he owes him an ounce of gold. To speak literally of a money price of gold, is just as if a person were to ask *how much tea he must give for a pound of tea.*"

* 24th June 1852.

I feel that I have perhaps laboured this point more
than is neeessary; but on the subject of money generally, and more especially on the nature and extent of
the coming changes in its value, there are a thousand
misconceptions abroad.\* I have resolved, therefore, to

* In an able lecture, containing many valuable facts, " On the
History and Statistics of Gold," delivered a short time ago at
the Museum of Practical Geology, by Mr Hunt, Keeper of the
Mining Records, the following passage occurs (p. 170) :—" Many
fears have been expressed lest the great influx of gold into this
country should produce a considerable difference in its value.  It
will be evident to all, that if gold, instead of being worth £4 an
ounce, as it is at present, should, from some extraordinary supply, suddenly fall to £3 an ounce, that every man possessed, say
of 100 sovereigns, would find their value sunk to £75; and those
who had incomes, say of £400 per annum, would discover to
their sorrow that they could only realize £300 worth of any other
article which the necessities of their existence might require in
exchange for gold."  I quote this in order to show you the errors
into which popular writers are apt to fall, from mixing up two
things which are quite distinct—namely, the *value* of gold and the
*price* of gold.  An influx of gold may reduce a £400 income to
£300 *in purchasing power*—may reduce the *value* of gold in relation to commodities by one-fourth; but no influx, however
great, can make the *price* of gold " fall to £3 an ounce."  No
wonder that a writer with such views of value should, from " the
study of the facts of history," deduce " the inference that it is
improbable any very extensive commercial changes will arise from

take nothing for granted, and beg that it may be impressed upon your mind at the outset, and kept steadily in view throughout the whole discussion, that whatever be the effects of the unparalleled supplies of gold now flowing in upon us from all quarters, no change whatever will take place upon *the money price of gold itself.*

the discovery of extraordinary quantities of gold in Australia, California, or elsewhere." The only historical documents that bear upon the *price* of gold are the Indentures of the Mint.

# LETTER VI.

## *Will the increased supplies of gold reduce the interest of money?*

THAT the present unprecedented importations of gold, if continued for many years longer, as they would seem likely to be, will produce the most momentous effects upon the condition of all ranks and classes of society, appears to be universally allowed. Men who differ upon every other subject are all but unanimous upon this. The exact nature of the effects likely to be produced, and the *modus operandi*, they do not very clearly see, but they are pretty well agreed that the more immediate consequence will be a *fall in the value of money*. Now, what is meant by a fall in the value of money? One man will tell you that by and by the gold contained in a sovereign will be worth only ten shillings, or may fall to half-a-crown—*that* error I trust I have sufficiently exposed in my last letter. Another will inform you that a fall in the value of money means *a reduction of the rate of interest,* and a consequent rise in the price of consols and annuities.  That is another prevalent misconception, which I shall endeavour to dispose of in my present letter.

That any general fall in the value of money, any diminution of its purchasing power, will affect interest and principal alike, and for that reason will not change the relation between them, would seem to be self-evident.  If, after the anticipated change, £100 will go no farther than £50 at present in the purchase of goods, it follows necessarily that £4, which we suppose to be the present interest of £100 for a year, will go no farther than £2.  Again, if a perpetual annuity of £3 cost at present £100, whatever diminution there may be in the purchasing power of the annuity will affect equally its price.  There is nothing, therefore, in the reason of the thing to lead us to expect a reduction of interest, or a rise in the funds.  Glut the market with gold, and reduce the value of money as you will, four will still bear the same proportion to 100 which it does at present.*

* Recent accounts inform us, that in California, where the pressure of gold upon the market has raised the wages of ordinary day labour to 100 dollars (or about £20) a-month, and wheat to

Suppose that in a year of scarcity, I borrow 1000 quarters of wheat, and engage to return that quantity the following year, with forty quarters, or 4 per cent. more, as an acknowledgment for the accommodation I have received, I could not with any reason urge upon the neighbour who had thus obliged me, that wheat being now more abundant and of less value, he ought to be content with twenty instead of forty quarters. He would answer me, of course, that forty bears the same proportion to 1000 this year that it did the last, and he might add, that if in consequence of greater abundance forty quarters have now come to exchange for less money, and less of every other commodity than formerly, that is a reason rather for increasing than for diminishing the per-centage return.

This reasoning, I think, must be considered conclusive. Locke and Montesquieu both committed an error in representing the rate of interest as governed by the amount of the circulating medium—an error which was afterwards detected and exposed by Hume. Interest,

a famine price, the interest of money, notwithstanding, is, or was very lately, 3 per cent. per month, or 36 per cent. per annum: And in South Australia, where the same pressure has raised wages and the quartern loaf, by from 200 to 300 per cent., the rate of interest ranges from 15 to 25 per cent.

as is clearly shown by Adam Smith,* depends not on
the numerical amount of money in circulation, but on
the general rate of profits and the amount of capital in
the market seeking investment. No doubt *during the
progress* of the great change which we seem now on the
eve of witnessing, an impetus will be given to trade in
all its departments; and while the influx of gold continues, the amount of capital for investment will be
increased, and the rate of profits in consequence temporarily depressed. More remittances, in the first instance, will be made in gold, and fewer in produce.
The reserves of the banks will be increased,† *loanable*
capital (so to speak) will for a time be more than usually
abundant, and interest will fall. But this effect will
be transient. The additional capital will not long be
kept floating, but will be sent abroad, or get absorbed
in the various departments of domestic production. It

---

* Wealth of Nations, book i. chap. ix.

† The stock of bullion in the issue department of the Bank of
England, in the first week of September in each of the last four
years, was as follows :—

|  |  |  |  |
|---|---|---|---|
| September 8, 1849, | . . | £13,918,000. |
| ... 2, 1850, | . . | 16,103,000. |
| ... 5, 1851, | . . | 13,707,000. |
| ... 4, 1852, | . . | 21,353,000. |

is the interest of no one to keep more of his capital in the shape of ready money than he has immediate occasion for. The fall of interest therefore, like its cause, will be temporary. It is only during the flowing of that tide of metallic wealth which is now setting in upon us, that we may expect this effect to be produced. When the tide is at the full, and the amount of money again becomes fixed, the effect will cease; and for this reason, that the effect does not depend upon the absolute amount of money, but upon the temporary depression of mercantile profits consequent upon the progressive increase of floating capital. All this was ably explained by Hume more than a hundred years ago, in his admirable *Political Discourses.**

* " The lowness of interest is generally ascribed to the plenty of money. But money, however plentiful, has no other effect, *if fixed*, than to raise the price of labour. Silver is more common than gold; and therefore you receive a greater quantity of it for the same commodities. But do you pay less interest for it? Interest in Batavia and Jamaica is at 10 per cent., in Portugal at 6; though these places, as we may learn from the prices of everything, abound much more in gold and silver than either London or Amsterdam. Were all the gold in England annihilated at once, and one and twenty shillings substituted for every guinea, would money be more plentiful or interest lower? No surely: We should only use silver instead of gold. Were gold rendered as common as copper; would money be more

Mr Tooke takes the same view of the subject :—
" When the amount of the currency," he observes,
plentiful or interest lower? We may assuredly give the same
answer. Our shillings would then be yellow and our halfpence
white ; and we should have no guineas. No other difference
would ever be observed. No alteration on commerce, navigation,
or interest ; unless we imagine that the colour of the metal is of
consequence. Now what is visible in those greater variations of
scarcity and abundance of the precious metals, must hold in all
inferior changes. If the multiplying gold and silver fifteen
times makes no difference, much less can the doubling or tripling
of them. All augmentation has no other effect than to heighten
the price of labour and commodities, and even this variation is
little more than a name. *In the progress towards these changes*,
the augmentation may have some influence by exciting industry ;
but after the prices are settled, suitable to the new abundance of
gold and silver, it has no manner of influence. An effect always
holds proportion with its cause. Prices have risen about four
times since the discovery of the Indies ; and 'tis probable gold
and silver have multiplied much more : But interest has not
fallen much above half. The rate of interest therefore is not
derived from the quantity of the precious metals. . . . The same
interest in all cases holds the same proportion to the sum. And
if you lent me so much labour and so many commodities ; by
receiving 5 per cent., you receive always proportionate labour
and commodities, however represented, whether by yellow or
white coin, whether by a pound or an ounce. 'Tis in vain therefore to look for the cause of the fall or rise of interest in the
greater or less quantity of gold and silver which is fixed in any
nation. . . . Those who have asserted that the plenty of money

" has become settled for any length of time, at a particular level, it is immaterial, as relates to the rate of
interest, whether the level of the currency be at one-
half or at double its former value. The rate of interest
will then be governed entirely by the supply of and
demand for capital, as resulting from circumstances independent of the currency. But," adds Mr Tooke, " it
cannot be too constantly borne in mind that every alteration in the amount of currency produces a temporary
effect upon the rate of interest." *

For the reasons which have been stated, then, we
must be prepared to expect a fall of interest during the
progress of the change which seems about to take place
in the value of money, and a corresponding advance of
the funds and rise in the money price of fixed incomes
and annuities, and also in the price of land, as affected
by the rate of interest, independently of the effects likely
to be produced on the money value of its produce.

And here I shall take the liberty to add an observation which has probably often been made before, but
which I do not remember to have met with elsewhere.

was the cause of low interest, seem to have taken a collateral effect
for a cause."—*Hume's Political Discourses*, 2d edit. p. 61-73.

    * Considerations on the State of the Currency, 2d edit. pp. 23, 24.

Of its soundness you must judge for yourself,—I set it down as a subject for inquiry, rather than as a received or accredited doctrine.

In economics, as in mechanics, we have action and reaction. In mercantile affairs that which in the first instance was a consequence becomes in its turn a cause, producing effects in an opposite direction, and the oscillation, if unchecked, continues and increases until a crisis or convulsion restores the equilibrium. Adam Smith tells us, that the rate of interest depends upon the average rate of mercantile profits, and that the rate of profits is regulated in a great measure by the relative amount of capital seeking investment. But is it not equally true that *the amount of capital for investment is in turn governed to a large extent by the rate of interest?*

To explain what I mean: Suppose the annual rent of a land estate to be £1000, and the common rate of interest, as in the reign of James the First, to be 10 per cent.—land, or fixed and durable capital, yielding £1000 per annum, would be worth £10,000, or ten years' purchase; it would be so, because a capital ten times greater than the rent annually received from the land, or the profits derived annually from the fixed capital, would, if invested in any other department, yield, at 10 per cent., an annual return equal to £1000. Again, suppose the common rate of interest reduced to 6 per cent., the value of the land or fixed capital would rise to £16,667, and for the same reason; or to 5 per cent., it would rise to £20,000; or to 4 per cent., £25,000; or to 3 per cent., £33,333; or to 2 per cent., £50,000; or to 1 per cent., £100,000.

Now it will be observed that with every per-centage reduction of the rate of interest, the value of land, or fixed capital, rises *in an increased ratio*. The reduction from 5 to 4 per cent. adds £5000 to the capital; but the reduction from 4 to 3 per cent. adds £8333; from 3 to 2 per cent., £16,667; and from 2 to 1 per cent., £50,000.

Sir Robert Peel estimated the land rental of the United Kingdom at £72,800,000.* This at 4 per cent., or twenty-five years' purchase, would make the gross value £1,820,000,000; but at 2 per cent. the value would be double that sum, or £3,640,000,000. The fall of interest in the same way increases not only the value of perpetual annuities (3 per cent. consols for example), but of dividends from canals, railways, or other property. Suppose I receive £500 per annum as my share of the profits of a canal or a railway, in which I

* Porter's Progress of the Nation, sec. vi. chap. ii.

hold 100 shares: if the market rate of interest upon investments were 4 per cent., the value of these shares would probably be £12,500; but if the common rate of interest be reduced to 2 per cent., the value of these shares might be doubled.

Thus the fall of interest raises the price of land and fixed capital; and as the holders of such property can either sell it for more money in the market, or borrow larger sums upon the security of it for investment in other departments when interest falls, over-speculation, over-trading, and a mercantile convulsion, are too frequently the consequence. Hence it is not the additional facility of obtaining loans from bankers by reason of the reduction of interest which alone leads to such convulsions, but the increased facility of borrowing upon the security of fixed capital and land, as enhanced in value by that very reduction. First of all, there is the action of the augmented capital upon the rate of interest; and then there is the reaction of the reduced rate of interest on the value of securities, land, and fixed capital, which leads to an increase of the evil, until a monetary crisis and a thousand bankruptcies clear the market of the undue proportion of floating capital with which for the time it is overcharged.

It is of great importance in economical science to attend to this law of action and reaction. For example, without entering upon the vexed question of *general gluts*, upon which so much has been written to so little purpose, it will probably be allowed that there are seasons when the market is overstocked with all, or most, of our staple manufactures, and when, in consequence, it becomes absolutely necessary to limit the supply, in order if possible to bring the actual up to the natural or remunerative prices. The usual rate of production cannot be continued. Thousands of labourers are thrown out of employment altogether, and the rest are perhaps employed during only half the day, or at reduced wages. The evil which the manufacturer has to contend with is a languid or inadequate demand, and the evil is increased by the very means taken to cure it. The consumption of all the other classes of the community, as compared with the consumption of the working classes, who form the great body of the people, is as nothing. Here, then, you have an overloaded market and ruinously low prices, because the supply is more than adequate to the demand; and at the very same moment, and as a consequence of this, you have a most ruinous diminution even of the or-

dinary demand, because the means of purchasing have
to a great extent been withdrawn from the working
classes—the great body of consumers. Prices, which
before were low, are now still farther reduced. A mercantile convulsion is the consequence ; and it is not till
half our traders and manufacturers have passed through
the Gazette, and the Market has been cleared of the
glut of commodities by sales effected without reference
to cost or profits, that the equilibrium between supply
and demand is restored, and trade regains a healthy
position.

Let me just add, that in this last case, the force of
the reaction would be greatly modified, were the labourers in their days of prosperity to exercise a little
more prudence, and deposit in the savings banks a fund
which could be made available for their support, and
enable them in some degree to continue their ordinary
rate of consumption when adverse times come round.
We should then have to contend with only the action
of an over-supply upon prices, without the added and
simultaneous evil of a contracted demand. But all this,
however important, is a digression from the main subject of our inquiry, to which I shall return in my next
letter.

# LETTER VII.

*Money a universal equivalent—its local value fluctuates—
its permanent value is regulated by the cost of obtaining
the metal which forms the standard—recent rise of wages
and prices in Australia.*

HAVING shown you that the present unprecedented influx of gold is not likely to affect the interest of money
otherwise than temporarily, and can have no effect at
all upon the *price* of the metal itself, I must revert
again to first principles, before I can fully and intel-
ligibly explain to you the consequences to commerce
and society which must result from the disturbance of
the equilibrium between the precious metals and other
commodities.

In my second letter, I showed you that money discharges two distinct functions; first, as a measure of
value; and, secondly, as an instrument of exchange; and
I undertook to prove to you, that no commodity can

discharge these functions accurately unless it possess intrinsic value. Money, which is a measure of value, unlike other measures, passes from hand to hand. It is a *universal equivalent,* and to constitute it an equivalent the standard must be composed of a material which is itself the product of labour and capital, like the other commodities whose value it measures, and whose exchange and distribution it facilitates.

Although it is a solecism to talk of the *price of gold* in a country where that metal forms the standard of money, gold like every thing else rises and falls *in value,* but its value is expressed not in money but in commodities. If a quarter of wheat, for example, which last year was exchanged for 246 grains of standard gold, or two pounds-sterling, can be exchanged this year for 369 grains, or three pounds-sterling, it is not more correct, although it is more common, to say that the price of wheat, or its value in relation to gold, has risen, than it is to say that the value of gold in relation to wheat has fallen. Diminish the supply of wheat, the amount of gold in circulation remaining the same, and you raise its money value—a determinate quantity of wheat will exchange for more gold than formerly. Increase the amount of gold, the supply of wheat remaining the same, and you produce exactly the same result—a determinate sum will exchange for less wheat than formerly.

Accustom yourself, therefore, to think of gold as a commodity which rises and falls in value like other things, but which has its value expressed, not in money, but in other products, rising in value as all other commodities fall in price, and falling in value as all other commodities rise in price. A general fall in the value of money, therefore, is just another expression for a general rise in the prices of all other commodities.

But the value of the precious metals in relation to commodities in any particular country, although liable to be influenced and disturbed by a change of the relative quantities of the circulating medium and commodities, is governed mainly, and their *permanent* value in the market of the world is governed exclusively, by their cost of production. If ten tons of copper and 500 tons of iron are the products of equal capitals, or an equal amount of labour, a ton of copper will exchange for fifty tons of iron. The supply of copper or iron, or the demand for either of these metals, may, for a time, be greater or less, and their relative value may be temporarily affected in consequence, but cost of production is the permanent regulator of their value.

The value of gold, as the metal forming the standard of money, is governed by exactly the same law. If a pound-weight of gold and two tons of lead are the products of equal capitals, or an equal amount of labour, a ton of lead will exchange for, or be worth, half-a-pound of gold, or £23, 7s. 3d.,—the sum into which, according to our mint regulations, half-a-pound of gold is coined. This is what Adam Smith calls the *natural price*, or, as I have elsewhere expressed it, the two metals exchanging for each other in these proportions, *their value is at par.** The cost of production, "the natural price, is as it were the central price to which the prices of all commodities are continually gravitating. Different accidents may sometimes keep them suspended a good deal above it, and sometimes force them down even somewhat below it. But whatever may be the obstacles which hinder them from settling in this centre of repose and continuance, they are constantly tending towards it."†

Diminish, for instance, the supply of lead in the market, the supply of gold remaining the same, and the

* Philosophy of Trade, book i. chap. iv.
† Wealth of Nations, book i. chap. vii.

market price of lead will for a time exceed the natural price; but the stimulus which the high price will give to increased production will very soon enlarge the supply, and bring its value back to par.   Increase the quantity of gold in the market, the supply of lead and of all other things remaining as before, and you will raise the money value of all things; but when general prices exceed or fall short of the natural price, an action on the foreign exchanges is created, which causes an efflux or influx of the metals to or from the countries where prices have been so enhanced or depressed, and brings general prices back to par.   Thus are the precious metals distributed among the different nations of the world, each receiving that portion which the state of its land, industry, and capital requires, and no more.*

* "Suppose four-fifths of all the money in Britain to be anni-hilated in one night, and the nation reduced to the same condition in this particular as in the reigns of the Harrys and Edwards, what would be the consequence?  Must not the price of all labour and commodities sink in proportion, and every thing be sold as cheap as in those ages?  What nation could then dispute with us in any foreign market, or pretend to navigate or to sell man-ufactures at the same price, which to us would afford sufficient profit?  In how little time therefore must this bring back the money which we had lost, and raise us to the level of all the neighbouring nations : where, after we have arrived, we imme-

This accounts sufficiently for the ease and quickness with which local inequalities in the distribution of the precious metals are redressed; but the phenomena which we are now witnessing, and about to witness, must be traced to a different source—namely, a great and marked

diately lose the advantage of the cheapness of labour and commodities; and the farther flowing in of money is stopped by our fulness and repletion. Again, suppose that all the money in Britain were multiplied fivefold in a night, must not the contrary effect follow? Must not all labour and commodities rise to such an exorbitant height, that no neighbouring nations could afford to buy from us, while their commodities, on the other hand, become so cheap in comparison, that in spite of all the laws which could be formed, they would be run in upon us, and our money would flow out, till we fall to a level with foreigners, and lose that great superiority of riches which had laid us under such disadvantages? Now it is evident that the same causes which would correct these exorbitant inequalities, were they to happen miraculously, must prevent their happening in the common course of nature, and must for ever in all neighbouring nations preserve money nearly proportioned to the art and industry of each nation. All water, wherever it communicates, remains always at a level. Ask naturalists the reason, they tell you that were it to be raised in any one place, the superior gravity of that part not being balanced, must depress it till it meets a counterpoise; and that the same cause which redresses the inequality when it happens must for ever prevent it, without some violent external operation."—*Hume's Political Discourses*, 2d edit. p. 82.

change in the cost of producing the metals in the
countries whence they are derived,—a cause which,
should it continue in operation, will by and by have
the effect of permanently changing the value of gold in
all the markets of the world. California and the Ural,
and our own Australian Colonies, are all pouring forth
their treasures, without any visible limit to their apparently inexhaustible supplies. Just look, for instance,
at the recent despatches of Mr Latrobe, Lieutenant-
Governor of Victoria, in which we are told that it has
already become necessary to the public service in the
colony to raise, by from 50 to 100 per cent., the salaries
and wages of all persons employed; that the wages of
the police, turnkeys, letter-carriers, &c., have been
raised from 4s. 6d. to 7s. and 8s. a-day, and the salaries
of clerks about 50 per cent. From the same document
we learn, that the rise of wages and prices has been
even larger in private employments. Labourers' wages
have risen from 5s. to 15s. and 20s. a-day. On artisans'
wages the increase is from 80 to 120 per cent. Men
cooks get £2 and £3 a-week; female servants have received an advance of 25 per cent. on the former wages.
The quartern loaf rose in price from 5d. in December
1850 to 1s. 4d., and even 1s. 8d. in December 1851;

meat doubled in price; bacon rose from 6d. to 2s. a-lb.; and on all the articles of domestic consumption the rise has been from 50 to 100 per cent. House-rent, hotel charges, cartage, boat-hire, have risen 50 per cent.; clothes, hardware, and furniture, 100 per cent.; saddlery is not to be got; and the prices of shoeing a horse have increased from 5s. to 25s.*

The reason of this extraordinary rise of wages and prices is obvious enough. If a labourer, who before could earn only 5s. a-day in tilling the soil or taking care of sheep, can upon an average earn 15s. or 20s. a-day in digging for gold, he will not (with some allowance probably for the uncertainty and greater hardship of the latter occupation) accept of lower wages in the one employment than he could get in the other. But labour being raised in price, commodities, which are the products of labour, must rise to a corresponding extent. Even Mr Ricardo, who teaches that wages have in general no effect upon price, allows that if wages are elevated by reason of a fall in the value of money, the money prices of all things must rise in consequence. The doctrine of Adam Smith, that a rise or

* Farther Papers relative to the recent Discovery of Gold in Australia, presented to Parliament, 14th June 1852, pp. 78, 79.

fall in the money price of goods, proceeding entirely from a change in the value of the precious metals, "must affect all goods *equally*, and raise or lower their prices *universally*," is not inconsistent with the inequalities exhibited by the phenomena we are now witnessing. Increase the supply of gold, and diminish its cost of production, *all commodities remaining as formerly*, and continuing of the same value *inter se*, and you undoubtedly raise the prices of all things in equal proportion. But in the instance we have been considering, all things have not remained as formerly. Hence the advance of price in the case of some commodities is greater than in that of others. But the rise in all the cases is nevertheless attributable to the change which has taken place in the value of money. This subject is explained by Colonel Torrens, with his usual clearness and ability, in a recent work.* "Adam Smith's principle," says Colonel Torrens, "is incontrovertibly, is self-evidently true, when considered in relation to the circumstances under which it is enunciated in the Wealth of Nations. It is self-evidently true that variations in the value of money must affect all commodities equally,

* Principles and Practical Operation of Sir Robert Peel's Act of 1844 Explained, &c., pp. 93, 94.

and raise or lower their prices universally, provided the values of commodities in relation to each other remain the same; but then it is self-evidently false that variations in the value of money must raise or lower the price of commodities equally and universally, when the values of commodities, in relation to each other, do not remain the same. Let the cost of obtaining money and the cost of producing corn be diminished one-half, and the price of corn will remain the same, while the prices of all other commodities will be doubled. Practically, the relative cost of producing commodities, and, as a necessary consequence, their value in relation to each other, is liable to constant fluctuation; therefore, practically, a fall in the value of money, while raising the prices of all commodities, the cost of producing which has remained unchanged, may be accompanied by a fall in the prices of those commodities, the cost of producing which has been lowered in a greater proportion than the cost of obtaining money."

# LETTER VIII.

*Laws which determine the permanent value of the precious metals—Opinions of Adam Smith, Mr Ricardo, Mr M<sup>c</sup> Culloch, and Mr James Mill.*

FROM what I have said in my last letter, you will see that there are four supposable causes to which a permanent and universal elevation or depression of the value of the precious metals can be attributed—namely, 1st, A change of the conditions under which the metals themselves are produced, without a corresponding change of the conditions under which commodities are produced. If the cost of producing the metals is diminished, general prices will rise, and *vice versa ;* that is to say, a larger quantity of gold or silver will be given for a determinate portion of any other commodity, and *vice versa.* 2d, An alteration of the conditions under which commodities generally are produced, without a corresponding change in the conditions under which gold and silver are produced. If the cost of producing all commodities be diminished—the cost of producing the metals being as before—a larger quantity of every commodity will be given in exchange for a determinate quantity of gold and silver, and *vice versa*,—or, which is the same thing, the price of commodities will fall, and the value of money will rise. 3d, An increase or diminution of the total amount of the precious metals in circulation, without a corresponding enlargement or abridgment of the total supply of commodities to be exchanged and circulated by their means; or, 4th, An increase or diminution of the supply of commodities, without a corresponding enlargement or abridgment of the amount of the precious metals in circulation.

These four supposable causes may be more shortly stated, and may indeed be reduced to two—namely, 1st, An alteration of the relative cost of producing commodities and the precious metals; or, 2d, A change in their relative quantities.

The problem which we are called upon to solve therefore is, which of the two supposable causes last stated is the true, proximate, and efficient cause of the permanent alterations which have occurred, and seem again likely to occur, in the relative value of money and commodities?

Before entering upon this inquiry, I may remark that the mere statement of the question shows the difficulty of proceeding by induction, or of applying to its solution what Lord Bacon has termed the *experimentum crucis*. For although in the case of commodities produced under a monopoly we frequently witness the phenomenon of an enlargement or abridgment of supply, without any change in the cost or conditions of production, we do not so frequently see this phenomenon thus isolated in the case of freely produced commodities. And again, which creates a still greater difficulty, we absolutely never see an alteration of the conditions under which commodities not subject to monopoly are produced, that is to say, an increase or diminution in their cost of production, without a corresponding addition to or abridgment of the supply. The necessity of viewing the phenomena in the concrete thus gives rise to a difficulty in the outset of the inquiry; and accordingly we find that our most eminent economists, although they substantially agree in the conclusion that the cost of producing the metals ultimately regulates the permanent value of money, differ somewhat in regard to the *modus operandi*. I shall give you their opinions as shortly as possible in their own words.

Adam Smith, who makes labour the foundation of the value of all commodities, makes it also the foundation of the relative value of gold and silver; but the enlargement or abridgment of the relative quantity, as resulting from their increased or diminished cost of production, he represents as the proximate cause of all disturbances of the equilibrium between money and commodities. "When more abundant mines are discovered," he says, "a greater quantity of the precious metals is brought to market, and the quantity of the necessaries and conveniences of life for which they must be exchanged being the same as before, equal quantities of the metals must be exchanged for smaller quantities of commodities. So far, therefore, as the increase of the quantity of the precious metals in any country arises from the increased abundance of the mines, it is necessarily connected with some diminution of their value."*

"Gold and silver," says Mr Ricardo, "like all other commodities, are valuable only in proportion to the quantity of labour necessary to produce them and bring them

---

* Wealth of Nations, book i. chap. xi.

to market. Gold is about fifteen times dearer than silver, not because there is a greater demand for it, nor because the supply of silver is fifteen times greater than that of gold, but solely because fifteen times the quantity of labour is necessary to procure a given quantity of it."*
In other parts of his works, particularly in his chapter on Foreign Trade, Mr Ricardo attributes a general rise or fall of prices to an enlargement or contraction of the numerical amount of money in circulation as the proximate cause; and this is still more broadly stated in the following passage : †—" If a mine of gold were discovered [in England or France], the currency of either country would be lowered in value in consequence of the increased quantity of the precious metals brought into circulation, and would therefore no longer be of the same value as that of other countries.  Gold and silver, whether in coin or in bullion, obeying the law which regulates all other commodities, would immediately become articles of exportation; they would leave the country where they were cheap for those countries where they were dear, and would continue to do so as long as the mine should prove productive, and till the

* Principles of Political Economy (M'Culloch's Edition), p. 213.
† Works, p. 264.

proportion existing between capital and money in each country before the discovery of the mine were again established, and gold and silver restored everywhere to one value." In this and similar passages, however, it will be observed that Mr Ricardo is speaking of the value of money in particular countries, and the causes of its influx and efflux, not of its general and permanent value in the market of the world, which he appears to set down as exclusively dependent upon cost of production.*

Mr M'Culloch—in this as in most other departments of the science, the able and faithful disciple of Mr Ricardo —has adopted the same view of the subject. " The value of all commodities which may be freely produced, and whose quantity may be increased proportionally to the increased demand for them, is in no degree dependent

---

* In a very able article which appeared in the Edinburgh Review for July 1843, to which I shall have occasion to refer more particularly hereafter, one object of the writer is to show, which he does very convincingly, " That the value of money, in so far as it is decided by intrinsic causes, does not depend *permanently* on the quantity of it possessed by a given community, or on the rapidity of its circulation, or on the prevalence of exchanges, or on the use of barter or credit, or, in short, on any cause whatever, excepting *the cost of its production*."

on the qualities they possess, but wholly on the cost of
their production, or on the amount of labour and capital
required to produce them and bring them to market.
Gold is not more valuable than iron, or lead, or tin,
because of its greater brilliancy, durability, or ductility,
but simply because an infinitely greater outlay of capital and labour is required to produce a given quantity
of gold, than is required to produce the same quantity
of either of these metals." After illustrating this proposition, he adds, " It is not meant by anything that
has now been stated, to deny that the value of gold
and silver is liable to be affected by variations in the
supply of and demand for them. It is difficult, however, to suppose that such variations can ever take place
to any great extent, unless they have been preceded by
a change in the cost of producing the metals. The in-
timate commercial relations that are now established
between the remotest quarters of the world have had
the effect to distribute the precious metals, so that their
value in any one country differs but little from their
value in others; and while their great durability pre-
vents any sudden diminution of their quantity, the immense surface over which they are spread, and the
various purposes to which they are applied, render the

effect of a considerable increase of supply on their value hardly sensible. All great and permanent variations in the value of the precious metals must therefore be occasioned by corresponding variations in the cost of their production."*

Mr Mill, while he arrives at the same conclusion, explains the matter somewhat differently. "In whatever degree," he says, "the quantity of money is increased or diminished, other things remaining the same, in that same proportion the value of the whole, and of every part, is reciprocally diminished or increased. This, it is evident, is a proposition universally true. Whenever the value of money has either risen or fallen (the quantity of goods against which it is exchanged and the rapidity of circulation remaining the same), the change must be owing to a corresponding diminution or increase of the quantity, and can be owing to nothing else. If the quantity of goods diminish while the quantity of money remains the same, it is the same thing as if the quantity of money had been increased; and if the quantity of goods be increased while the quantity of money remains unaltered, it is the same thing as if

* M‘Culloch's Edition of Wealth of Nations, note ix., vol. iv. pp. 203, 204, 205.

the quantity of money had been diminished. Similar changes are produced by any alteration in the rapidity of circulation."* In a subsequent chapter, Mr Mill says correctly, that "it is the cost of production which determines the value of gold and silver as of other ordinary productions," and that the value of the metal determines the quantity of money. But then when he comes to explain *the mode* in which the quantity of money is regulated by the value of the metal, he appears to fall into the same error which Mr Blake and other writers had committed, in representing the value of the coin as liable to rise above or fall below that of the bullion which it contains.†

* Mill's Elements of Political Economy, 2d edit., pp. 128, 129.

† " It is evident that individuals possessed of bullion, will desire to convert it into coins, only when it is their interest to do so ; that is, when their bullion, converted into coins, will be more valuable to them than in the shape of bullion. This can only happen when the coins are peculiarly valuable, and when the same quantity of metal, in the state of coin, will exchange for more than in the state of bullion. As the value of the coins depends upon the quantity of them, it is only when they are small in quantity that they have this value. It is the interest of individuals, when coins are thus high in value, to carry bullion to be coined ; but by every addition to the number of the coins, the value of them is diminished ; and at last the value of the metal in the

His reasoning upon this subject, as I have shown you in my fifth letter, involves a complete fallacy. You may as well talk of weighing water in water in order to obtain its specific gravity, as of estimating the value of bullion in coins, or of coins in bullion. As long as the coins are perfect according to the standard, and the mint regulations order, as ours do, forty lbs. troy of standard gold bullion to be coined, instantly and gratuitously, into 1869 sovereigns, a fortieth part of this quantity, or one pound troy, will always exchange for

coins, above the bullion, becomes too small to afford a motive for carrying bullion to be coined. If the quantity of money, therefore, should at any time be so small as to increase its value above that of the metal of which it is made, the interest of individuals operates immediately, in a state of freedom, to augment the quantity. It is also possible for the quantity of money to be so large, as to reduce the value of the metal in the coin, below its value in the state of bullion: in that case, the interest of individuals operates immediately to reduce the quantity. If a man has possessed himself of a quantity of the coins, containing, we shall say, an ounce of the metal, and if these coins are of less value than the metal in bullion, he has a direct motive to melt the coins, and convert them into bullion; and this motive continues to operate till, by the reduction of the quantity of money, the value of the metal in that state is so nearly the same with its value in bullion, as not to afford a motive for melting."—*Mill's Elements of Political Economy*, 2d edit., pp. 131, 133.

£46, 14s. 6d.; and the twelfth part of a pound troy, or an ounce, will consequently always exchange for £3, 17s. 10½d. Hence coin and bullion will continue of precisely the same value in relation to commodities, whether the circulation upon the whole amount to one hundred pounds or to one hundred millions of pounds. The error which Mr Mill, in common with Mr Thornton and Mr Blake, has thus fallen into, is avoided by Mr J. S. Mill, whose opinions I propose to examine at some length in my next letter. My object at present is to show you, that the eminent economists, to whose works I have referred, agree in representing the cost of producing the precious metals as the ultimate regulator of their value, and that although they differ some-what as to the *modus operandi*, the opinion most generally received appears to be, that cost regulates relative quantity, and raises or depresses the value of gold and silver through the agency of supply and demand. This, as you will afterwards see, has an important bearing on the question—*When* are the present changes likely to produce their effect?

# LETTER IX.

*Laws which determine the value of the precious metals— Opinions of Mr J. S. Mill—Potential and actual enlargements of supply—Phenomena of prices in Australia.*

THE very able and elaborate work of Mr John Stuart Mill, entitled *Principles of Political Economy*, I cannot recommend too strongly to your perusal and study. You will find in it, along with much valuable original matter, all the received doctrines of the science, as embodied in the writings of Adam Smith and his successors, clearly stated, logically reasoned upon, and often very happily illustrated. Among other things, you will find a very clear exposition of the doctrine of value, as dependent on cost of production.

Mr Mill states correctly that cost of production frequently operates upon price, through *potential* and not actual alterations of the supply. "The latent influence,"

he says, " by which the values of things are made to
conform in the long-run to the cost of production, is
the variation that would otherwise take place in the
supply of the commodity. The supply would be increased if the thing continued to sell above the ratio of
its cost of production, and would be diminished if it fell
below that ratio. But we must not therefore suppose
it to be necessary that the supply should *actually* be
either diminished or increased. Suppose that the cost
of production of a thing is cheapened by some mechanical
invention, or increased by a tax. The value of the thing
would in a little time, if not immediately, fall in the
one case, and rise in the other; and it would do so,
simply because if it did not, the supply would in the
one case be increased, until the price fell, in the other
diminished, until it rose."* All this I conceive to be
thoroughly sound doctrine.

But, then, when Mr Mill comes to treat of the precious metals as the materials of money, he arrives at the
conclusion that cost of production does not operate upon
value through potential, but only through actual alterations of the supply: " Since the value of money," he

* Mill's Principles of Political Economy, book iii. chap iii.
sec. ii.

observes, "really conforms, like that of other things,
although more slowly, to its cost of production, some
political economists have objected altogether to the statement that the value of money depends on its quantity,
combined with the rapidity of circulation; which, they
think, is assuming a law for money that does not exist
for any other commodity, when the truth is that it is
governed by the very same laws.   To this we may
answer, in the first place, that the statement in question
assumes no peculiar law.  It is simply the law of demand
and supply, which is acknowledged to be applicable
to all commodities, and which, in the case of money, as
of most other things, is controlled, but not set aside, by
the law of cost of production, since cost of production
would have no effect on value, if it could have none on
supply.   But, secondly, there really is, in one respect,
a closer connexion between the value of money and its
quantity, than between the value of other things and their
quantity.   The value of other things conforms to the
changes in the cost of production, without requiring, as a
condition, that there should be any actual alteration of the
supply—the *potential alteration is sufficient;* and if there
even be an actual alteration, it is but a temporary one,
except in so far as the altered value may make a differ-

ence in the demand, and so require an increase or diminution of supply, as a consequence, not a cause, of the alteration in value. Now this is also true of gold and silver, considered as articles of expenditure for ornament and luxury; *but it is not true of money.* If the cost of production of gold were reduced one-fourth, by the discovery of more fertile mines, it might happen that there would not be more of it bought for plate, gilding, or jewellery, than before; and if so, though the value would fall, the quantity extracted from the mines for these purposes would be no greater than previously. *Not so with the portion used as money;* that portion *could not fall in value one-fourth, unless actually increased one-fourth;* for, at prices one-fourth higher, one-fourth more money would be required to make the accustomed purchases; and if this were not forthcoming, some of the commodities would be without purchasers, and prices could not be kept up. Alterations, therefore, in the cost of production of the precious metals, do not act upon the value of money *except just in proportion as they increase or diminish its quantity;* which cannot be said of any other commodity."*

* Principles of Political Economy, book iii. chap. ix. sec. iii.— The italics in the above quotation are mine, not Mr Mill's.

I make no apology for quoting this passage at length, because the subject, notwithstanding it has something of a metaphysical and speculative air, is one of supreme practical importance at this moment, involving, as I shall afterwards show you, no less an issue than, whether the great changes which the coming reduction of the value of money is likely to produce on commerce, and the condition of all classes of society, may be expected to take place immediately; or, as in the case of the increased supplies of silver from the American mines in the sixteenth century, may be looked for some eighty or ninety years after the discovery of the more abundant deposits. This problem is one of great interest, as well as of considerable scientific difficulty; and having seen reason to modify, to some extent, the opinions which I formerly entertained upon the subject,—opinions very much in accordance with those so well and clearly expressed by Mr Mill,—I am the more anxious to bestow upon it that careful treatment which its great and urgent importance demands.

I am still far from asserting that the value of money has no connexion with its relative quantity. On the contrary, I maintain that its relative scarcity or abundance, by the temporary influence thereby exerted upon prices, mainly regulates its distribution among the various countries of the world, causing an efflux of the metals from countries where they are comparatively abundant, and, for that reason, comparatively of little value, and an influx of them into countries where they happen to be relatively scarce, and therefore relatively dear.  I have not altered my opinions upon that subject; but I confess that farther reflection, and the observation of passing phenomena, have gone far to convince me, that there is no good ground for concluding, with Mr Mill, that gold and silver, considered as the materials of money, differ in this respect from other commodities, or that a higher or lower cost of production produces no alteration of their value, *potentially* or otherwise, than through an enlargement or abridgment of their actual supply.

There would seem to be no reason either in theory or in fact for adopting such a conclusion.  Suppose a country where gold and silver are both produced, where trade is free, where any one may engage in either employment, or retire from both, if he thinks proper, where competition is unlimited and the supply inexhaustible. A gives B fifteen ounces of silver in exchange for one ounce of gold, both being the products of equal capitals, or an equal amount of labour. Why does A do so? Why does he give neither more nor less than fifteen ounces of silver for one ounce of gold? The reason is, *because* A, by employing in another department the same amount of labour and capital which produced the silver, can himself procure an ounce of gold. B, for the same reason, will not give more than one ounce of gold in exchange for fifteen ounces of silver, because B, by applying the same amount of labour and capital which produced the gold to the production of silver, can himself procure fifteen ounces of that metal. Theoretically therefore it is not necessary to assume an actual increase or diminution of the supply of either metal.

Again, suppose that an equal amount of labour and capital is required to produce twenty quarters of wheat and ten ounces of gold, a quarter of wheat will exchange for, or be worth, half-an-ounce of gold, or, supposing our mint regulations to be observed, the price of wheat will be 38s. 11d. a-quarter. But suppose again, that, by the discovery of new and more abundant mines, equal capitals will produce twenty ounces of gold and no more wheat than formerly, a quarter of the grain, in these altered circumstances, will exchange for, or be worth, a whole ounce of the metal; or the price of wheat will be double what it formerly was, or 77s. 10d. a-quarter. In order to account for this elevation of price, it is not necessary to assume an intermediate enlargement of the supply of coined gold or money. The case is this : I am possessed of a given amount of capital ; that capital will produce either a quarter of wheat or an ounce of gold. I am free to employ this capital as I choose. I may devote it either to mining or to agriculture, as I think most for my interest. Every other member of the community is equally free to choose between the two employments. Some will devote their capital to the one, some to the other. The miner knows this, and he knows also that were he to demand more than a quarter of wheat for an ounce of gold, no one would give it, *because* every one possesses the *power* to procure this quantity of the metal by a similar application of his capital or his labour. It is not necessary to suppose an actual transference of labour or capital, or an actual enlargement of the supply of either commodity. The *potentiality*, so to speak, the power, the option, is enough. If it be objected that to barter gold bullion for wheat is a different thing from exchanging wheat for gold coin, I have only to remind you, that I take it for granted as part of my hypothesis that there is a mint free and open to all, and under proper regulations, as well as the most perfect freedom of trade. Equal weights of coin and bullion of standard fineness being the same thing, if a quarter of wheat exchange for an ounce of gold, it will also exchange for £3, 17s. 10½d., or else things which are equal to the same are *not* equal to one another.

If you are not convinced by the hypothetical cases which I have put, just look at the rise of prices which has already taken place in Australia, where no mint has yet been established; where coined gold can only be procured from Europe; where bankers take jealous care of their issues of paper upon hypothecations of unassayed gold; and where, in consequence, a scarcity of the circulating medium has till lately been experienced. Yet there, we are told, the quartern loaf, after an abundant harvest, sells already for four times its former price. I ask, Why is this? Why has the price of labour in all departments risen so prodigiously? Why will the Melbourne policeman no longer remain at his post, or the jailer retain his keys, unless bribed by double or triple their former wages? *Because* by going to Mount Alexander, seventy miles off, and digging for gold, they find upon an average they can earn double ·or triple their former wages, with a handsome addition to compensate the uncertainty and hardship of their new employment. Why does the farmer pay 25s. instead of 5s. to the blacksmith for shoeing his horse, or to the saddler five times the former price for his harness? *because* the blacksmith and the saddler, each of them knows that he has the *power*, by deserting his own employment, and betaking himself to mining, to earn more than five times his former gains. Why, again, does the blacksmith pay four times the old price for his bacon? because the food of pigs, like the food of men, has been quadrupled in price; and why has food so risen in price? because the farmer, the market gardener, the grazier, the shepherd, the ploughman, the miller, the baker, the butcher, all who are in any way concerned in the raising of food, have the *power* of obtaining more money in a given time and with a given capital, by becoming diggers and washers of gold in the apparently inexhaustible fields now laid open to their industry, than they could have obtained in the same time and with an equal capital by carrying on their old trades at the former scale of prices.*

* " The openings for the agricultural labourer and the master or journeyman tradesman," says Mr Fairfax, " are astonishing.

For these reasons, it would seem to me that it cannot be maintained that the potential supply of gold, where

I will only mention one instance. It was told me by the Rev. Mr Mackenzie, a fellow-passenger from Sydney to England, and I am sure is only a specimen of the increase in the price of all kinds of handicraft. He says, ' Happening to break part of the harness of one of the horses I was driving, I desired my servant to carry the broken part to a saddler's shop, in order to get it mended. I accompanied the man. We travelled from shop to shop, until we had visited three or four of them, before we found a *man* in any of them ; all the men having gone to the diggings, the shops were left under the charge of their wives or daughters. At last we reached a saddler's shop in which I saw a little boy of nine or ten years of age, who said he thought he could mend the broken harness, and he did so in a few minutes. I stood looking at him while at work, and when he had finished I asked him what was to pay, expecting that he would say " one shilling." His reply however was, " Half-a-crown, sir, if you please." I said, " That is a very high charge, my little boy, for the few stitches it only cost you."—" But, sir," said this pocket edition of human nature, " you must consider that all the men have gone to the diggings, and that *we* who stay at home to do the work of the public must charge accordingly." The logic was conclusive ; my mouth was stopped, and my purse was opened. I paid the 2s. 6d., and went away convinced that those who stay at home and stick to their trades will largely participate in the profits of the gold digger. In January last, I was paying 30s. a-week, or at the rate of £78 a-year, with board, to a bullock-driver, whom I could have hired last year for about £30 a-year. When this man's time with

gold is the standard of money, does not of itself, and without the instrumentality of an extended currency, directly and instantly cause an elevation of general prices. That an enlarged currency, *without* any change in the cost of producing the material of money, will temporarily raise prices, and cause money to flow from one country to another till it finds its level, I cannot for a moment doubt. But that a reduction of the cost of production, even without such enlargement, has a direct independent action, would seem as little to be questioned. That an enlargement of the circulation will, under such circumstances, immediately follow the reduction of cost, as it is now doing in Australia,* must be regarded as a certain consequence. All that

me expired, he was offered £3 a-week, or at the rate of £156 a-year, with board, for driving bullocks between Melbourne and Mount Alexander. I know a journeyman carpenter, who was at the same time offered £4 a-week, with board, and constant employment, which he refused—then went to the diggings.' "—See a pamphlet entitled *The Colonies of Australia*, &c., by John Fairfax, Esq., joint proprietor and joint editor of the Sydney Morning Herald, pp. 47, 48.

* Since the accounts to which I have referred were received, 2,000,000 of sovereigns have been sent from this country to Australia, besides the sums taken out by emigrants.—See *Times* of 13th Sept. 1852.

I contend for is, that it *is* a consequence and not a cause.

I have said that the rise and fall in the local value of gold will cause it to flow backwards and forwards till it finds its *level;* but you must never forget that the cost of obtaining gold to every nation which employs that metal as the material of its money *is that level*—the point about which the value oscillates—the " centre of repose and continuance;" and that taking the world at large as one great market, nothing will universally and permanently either elevate or depress the value of the precious metals, but a permanent change in the conditions of their production.

But if this be so, you will say why did the gold and silver of America, which was discovered in Henry the Seventh's time, produce no very sensible effect upon general prices in Europe until about the middle of the reign of Elizabeth, ninety years afterwards? That is a very important, as well as a very difficult question, and I propose in the next eight letters to attempt its solution in the only way in which it can be solved—namely, by a careful examination of historical facts.

# LETTER X.

*American mines and European prices—State of the argument.*

BEFORE involving you in a multiplicity of figures and details with reference to the prices of so remote a period as that which intervened between the first discovery of the West Indies in 1492, and the general rise of prices in Europe which began about 1574, and continued till about 1636, according to Adam Smith, or 1650, according to Baron Humboldt, who upon this subject is perhaps the better authority, it is necessary to give you a clue to the labyrinth, by a short preliminary statement of the argument.

I propose to examine, as minutely as the scanty materials which are accessible will permit, the state of the circulating medium and prices during,

1st, The period which immediately preceded the discovery of America.

2d, The period which intervened between 1492 and 1545, when the great silver mines of the Cerro de Potosi began to discharge their treasures upon the markets of Europe.

3d, The period from the discovery of Potosi till 1574, when the process of amalgamation came into general use in the silver-producing countries; and,

4th, The period between 1574, when the first marked elevation of general prices began, and 1650, when, according to Humboldt, the continued enhancement of prices would appear to have ceased.

The state of the argument, then, is this : If during the *second* period—the period which immediately succeeded the discovery of the American treasures—we find that a considerable addition was made to the stock of the precious metals which had previously circulated in the commercial world, with little or no augmentation of general prices, this will afford a presumption against the conclusions of those who assert, that the mere increase of the quantity of the metals specifically caused the elevation of prices which afterwards took place.

Again, if during the *third* period—the period which succeeded the discovery of Potosi—when supplies of silver of a magnitude till then unheard of were thrown upon the market, and continued for many years to flow from the new to the old world, no very marked or sensible rise of general prices followed, the presumption to which I before adverted will be much strengthened and fortified.

And again, if during the *fourth* period—that which followed the general adoption of the process of amalgamation—the continued increase of the supply of silver (unlike what took place in the two former periods) *was* accompanied with a great and permanent rise of prices, we have what I think may be accounted very strong presumptive evidence that the elevation of prices which then took place was attributable to a cause peculiar to this fourth period—namely, the diminished cost of producing silver; and that the increase of supply, instead of being a cause, was simply a collateral effect.

Farther: If during the century which succeeded 1650, when prices are supposed to have reached their greatest elevation, still greater additions were made to the supply of silver than any which had preceded, *without* any material change in the cost of production, and if at the same time it appear that general prices did not exceed those of the immediately preceding period; and, *lastly*, if after 1750 a *second reduction of the cost of production* was followed by a *second general rise of prices* in Europe, then it humbly appears to me that there will be not a probability merely, but certain and conclusive proof, that the elevation of prices in both instances, and their continuance at the higher level, were attributable, not to increased supply, but diminished cost; and that the argument will then be as complete as the nature of the case admits of.

I say as the nature of the case admits of; because, as I formerly remarked, although we sometimes witness the phenomenon of an enlarged supply apart from any diminution of cost, we never in the case of a commodity not produced under a monopoly, see a reduction of cost which is not immediately followed by an enlargement of supply. The discovery of more productive mines is in fact another expression for reduction of cost, because if the mines did not produce more of the metals with the same expenditure of labour, they would *not* be more productive.

In digging for alluvial gold or washing auriferous sands, the metal is almost always found in its virgin state, and sometimes purer than our mint standard. Cost depends, therefore, almost entirely on the quantity produced by a given amount of manual labour, or man-

ual labour assisted by the rudest and most simple mechanical appliances.   But with silver—the metal with
which we are now more immediately concerned—the
case is different.   That metal is almost never found in
its pure or native state, but in combination with other
metals or mineral substances, and requires not only
labour, but machinery more or less complicated, and
chemical and metallurgical processes, implying the use
of expensive materials, to separate it from the ore, and
refine it sufficiently for the purposes of the mint or the
silversmith.

Silver in this respect more resembles iron, the cost
of which, as we all know, depends on the expense and
proximity of fuel, and other circumstances, quite as
much as upon the abundance of the ore.   That cost of
production is the permanent regulator of the value of
iron no one can doubt for a moment.   Just look at the
effects of the improved method, first suggested I believe
by Mr Neilson of Glasgow, and put in practice at the
Clyde Iron Works, for increasing the product of iron
with the same expense of materials, and which consists
in previously heating the air thrown into the furnace,
in order to accelerate combustion.   When the first experiments were tried in 1830, the air was heated to

300° Fahrenheit. In 1831, Mr Dixon of the Calder Iron Works substituted raw coal for the coke which had previously been used as fuel, at the same time heating the air to 600° Fahrenheit. This experiment was completely successful; and the result is, that three times as much iron is now made by the use of a given weight of coal than formerly;* and this and other improvements have reduced the price of iron (and consequently its value in relation to all other commodities) to less than one-third of what it was in the last century.

Similar effects followed the introduction, towards the end of the sixteenth century, of the improved method of separating silver from its ores by amalgamation with mercury. Silver being then the standard of our money, as gold is now, could not change in *price*, but its value in relation to all other commodities fell to a half, a third, and ultimately a fourth of what it had previously been—that is to say, the value of all commodities estimated in silver was doubled, tripled, and ultimately quadrupled. I shall return to this subject hereafter, but I mention it now, that you may not be misled by a false analogy. Gold is a metal which, when extracted

* Paper by Dr Clark of Aberdeen—Proceedings of Royal Society of Edinburgh, 2d Feb. 1835.

from the earth or washed from the sands, can be made almost instantly available ; the expense of producing it is mainly the manual labour of digging for it; and we shall, I fear, grossly deceive ourselves, if we imagine that twenty or thirty years must elapse, as in the case of the silver of Potosi, before it produces its effect upon prices.

# LETTER XI.

*State of the circulating medium, and prices of labour and commodities anterior to the discovery of America.*

HAVING made these preliminary observations, which I trust will sufficiently explain to you the scope and tendency of my argument, I shall devote this letter to the task of giving you as correct an idea as I am able of the general state of the circulating medium and prices during,

1st, The period immediately anterior to the discovery of America.

Mr Jacob, in his valuable History of the Precious Metals, calculates that the stock of gold and silver in circulation in Europe at the time of the discovery of America did not exceed £34,000,000, and that the annual additions then made to it did no more than supply the annual consumption.*

* Jacob's History of the Precious Metals, vol. ii. p. 53.

Of general prices prior to the discovery of America, the notices are so scanty, that I shall take a range of a century and a half nearly, beginning with 1350, when the *Statute of Labourers* (25th Edward III.) was passed. A destructive pestilence had just devastated England in common with the rest of Europe, carrying off nearly one-third of the whole inhabitants, and this statute was passed for the unjust and impolitic purpose of repressing the rising price of labour consequent on the diminution in the numbers of the people. This statute enacted, that " master carpenters, masons, tilers, and other coverers of houses, were not to take more than 3d. per day, and others but 2d. ; master masons of freestone, 4d., and other masons 3d., and their servants 1½d. per day; a reaper the first week of August, 2d.,—all without diet."*

* Anderson's History of Commerce, vol. i. p. 330.

In 1350, a pound weight of silver being coined into £1, 2s. 6d., the following would be the rates nearly in money of our times, estimating silver in our present gold coins at 5s. an ounce :—

| | | | |
|---|---|---|---|
| Master carpenters, &c., per day, | . . | £0 | 0 | 8 |
| Common artificers, nearly | . . . . | 0 | 0 | 5½ |
| Master masons, nearly | . . . . | 0 | 0 | 10¾ |
| Other masons, | . . . . . . | 0 | 0 | 8 |
| Their servants, | . . . . . | 0 | 0 | 4 |
| Reapers, | . . . . . . . | 0 | 0 | 5½ |

From 1339 to 1416, the average price of the quarter of wheat (in money of our time) appears to have been £1, 5s. 9⅓d. The average from 1423 to 1451, £1, 1s. 3⅓d.*

Bishop Fleetwood tells us, that in 1439 " a single clergyman might support himself with decency for £5 per annum,"†—a sum equal to £10 of the money of our time. The qualification of a justice of the peace was £20 per annum, equal to £40 of our money.‡ In 1442, Henry VI. settled lands for the maintenance of five Oxford scholars, at the rate of 10d. each per week,§ or 20d. of our present money.

The average price of wheat for the thirty-nine years ending with 1491, or rather the prices of such of those years as Fleetwood has recorded in his Chronicon Preciosum, when reduced to money of our time, does not exceed 14s. 1d.

The rate of wages in 1446 is thus noticed in the Chronicon Preciosum :—" A bailif of husbandry in England, at this time, had a yearly salary, besides his diet,

---

* See Table appended to Wealth of Nations (M'Culloch's Edition) vol. i. pp. 414, 415.

† Anderson's History of Commerce, vol. i. p. 459.    ‡ Ib.

§ Ib. vol. i. p. 464.

of £1, 3s. 4d.; also 5s. for his clothing yearly. A common servant in husbandry 15s. The chief carter and shepherd £1 yearly, with his diet, and 4s. each for clothing. A woman servant 10s., with diet, and for her clothing 4s. Moreover, a free mason, or master carpenter, had 4d. per day, and his diet; and without diet 5½d. per day. A master tiler, slater, rough mason, &c., with diet, 3d.; without diet, 4½d. A woman labourer 2½d., and diet; and without diet, 4½d.*

In 1465, " Edward IV. grants to the Lady Margaret, his sister (afterwards Duchess of Burgundy), an annual

* Anderson's History of Commerce, vol. i. p. 468.

A pound weight of silver being then coined into £1, 10s., the following would be the rates in money of the present day, taking silver, as before, at 5s. an ounce :—

| | | | |
|---|---|---|---|
| Bailif's wages, yearly, . . . . | £2 | 6 | 8 |
| „ clothing, . . . . . . | 0 | 10 | 0 |
| Servant in husbandry, yearly, . . . | 1 | 10 | 0 |
| Carter and shepherd, wages of each, yearly, . | 2 | 0 | 0 |
| „ clothing, each, . . | 0 | 8 | 0 |
| Woman servant, yearly, . . . . . | 1 | 0 | 0 |
| Free mason, &c., per day, with diet, . . | 0 | 0 | 8 |
| „ without diet, . . | 0 | 0 | 11 |
| Slater, rough mason, &c., per day, with diet, | 0 | 0 | 6 |
| „ without diet, | 0 | 0 | 9 |
| Woman labourer, wages per day, with diet, . | 0 | 0 | 5 |
| „ without diet, | 0 | 0 | 9 |

allowance of 400 merks [equal at present to 800 marks, or £533], for her clothes and the other necessaries of her body, suitable to the dignity of our kingdom, ourself, and her, and for wages and other expenses of the servants attending her; which annual allowance she shall enjoy until we can provide for her properly by a suitable marriage."*

In 1470, seven Spanish vessels, bound for Flanders, having been captured by English ships, the Spanish owners complain to Henry VI., who had now remounted the throne, exhibiting upon oath the burden and value of their ships, and the prices which their merchandise would have yielded in Flanders.

The catalogue is curious.

A ship of 100 tons, with her furniture,
valued at . . . . . £107, 10s.
Do. 70 tons, at . . . 70.
,, 120 ,, ,, . . . 110.
,, 110 ,, ,, . . . 140.
,, 40 ,, ,, . . . 70.
,, 110 ,, ,, . . . 150.
,, 120 ,, ,, . . . 180.

* Anderson's History of Commerce, vol. i. p. 485.

Their Bourdeaux wine, they swear, would have yielded in Flanders £5 per tun—their "Roman and bastard wines," £4—their iron, £4, 10s. per ton.* A pound of silver was at this time coined into £1, 17s. 6d.

In 1474, the daily pay of knights in the army was 2s. ; men-at-arms, 1s. ; archers, 6d. ; a duke's pay, 13s. 4d. ; an earl's, 6s. 8d. ; a baron's, 4s. ; the king's body physician, 2s. ; surgeons in the army, 1s. each.†

In 1495, three years after the discovery of the West Indies, a statute was passed to regulate wages, from which it appears that the price of common day labour was 4d. or 4½d., without diet, equal to 6d. or 6¾d. of our present money.‡

These scattered notices will give you some general idea of the scale of prices in England prior to the discovery of America; and in my next letter, I shall proceed to contrast these with such notices as I can find of the prices which prevailed both before and after the discovery of the rich mines of Potosi, but before the introduction of the process of amalgamation, the discovery of the quicksilver mines of Huancavelica, and the consequent fall in the cost of producing silver.

* Anderson's History of Commerce, vol. i. p. 496.    † Ib. p. 502.
‡ Sir F. M. Eden's State of the Poor, vol. iii. p. 89.

# LETTER XII.

*American mines and European prices—period from 1492 to the discovery of Potosi in 1545.*

CONTRASTING such notices as we have of prices in England, between 1492 and 1545, with those of the period we have already had under review, you will find that the money value of commodities fell rather than rose, notwithstanding the annual supplies of gold and silver furnished by America to the markets of Europe. According to Humboldt,[*] the mean annual supply of the precious metals from 1492 to 1500 amounted to £52,083, and from 1500 to 1545 to £625,000, giving a total for these fifty-three years of £28,541,664,—a sum not far short of the whole amount previously in circulation in Europe, and which Mr Jacob supposes to have been about equal to the annual consumption.

[*] Essai Politique sur la Nouvelle Espagne, liv. iv. chap. xi.

As far as mere increase of supply therefore is concerned, we should be prepared to expect at least *some*
enhancement of general prices.   But the reverse seems
to have been the case.   Unfortunately, of the fifty-three
years in question, in only six have the prices of wheat
been preserved, viz. :—

|  | Price per quarter in money of that time. | Price in money of the present time. |
|---|---|---|
| 1494, . . . | £0  4  0 | £0  6  0 |
| 1496, . . . | 0  4  0 | 0  5  0 |
| 1497, . . . | 1  0  0 | 1  11  0 |
| 1499, . . . | 0  4  6 | 0  6  0 |
| 1504, . . . | 0  5  8 | 0  8  6 |
| 1521, . . . | 1  0  0 | 1  10  0 |
|  |  | 6 \| £4  6  6 |
| | Average, | £0  14  5 |

Any conclusions drawn from so limited an average
of years must no doubt be very unsatisfactory.   Still,
as far as this average goes, it certainly by no means
countenances the idea that an elevation of prices was
a consequence of the enlarged supplies of the precious
metals.

Unfortunately we have no notices of the price of ordinary day labour in the reign of Henry the Seventh, subsequent to that in 1495, which I quoted in my last letter, and none at all in the reigns of Henry VIII., Edward VI., and Mary. In 1514, the Chronicon Preciosum sets down the daily pay of a master ship-wright at 5d. with diet, and 7d. without; a hewer, with diet, 4d., and without diet 6d.; and an able clincher the same.* In money of the present time these wages would amount to 6d., 7½d., and 9d.; and they do not much exceed those specified in the statute of labourers passed 164 years earlier.

In *Rymer's Fœdera*,† we have the catalogue of goods restored, in 1530, by Henry VIII., to Cardinal Wolsey. Among other matters, we have eighty horses, with their furniture, valued at £150, or £1, 17s. 6d. each, equal at present to £2, 16s. 3d. Four mules for the saddle, with furniture, valued at £60, or £15 each, equal now to £22, 10s. Six mules for carriage, valued at £40, or £6, 13s. 4d. each, equal in our money to £10. Sixty-two oxen, valued at £80, or £1, 5s. 9¾d. each, equal at present to £1, 18s. 8½d.; and, lastly, eighty sheep,

* Anderson's History of Commerce, vol. ii. p. 29.
† xiv. 375.

valued at £12, or 3s. each, equal in money of our day to 4s. 6d.

As far as these estimates are any criterion of general prices, we may compare them with those of sheep and oxen in a list of prices sanctioned by Edward II. and his council, upon a petition from the English parliament in 1315, when it was enacted that the best ox not fed with grain should be sold for 16s., equal to £2, 8s. of our money; and if fed with corn, at 24s. at most, equal to £3, 12s. at present; a fat-wether unshorn for 20d., equal now to 5s.; and if shorn 14d., equal in money of our day to 3s. 6d.*

These prices appear in those early days to have been considered moderate and reasonable; and yet they exceed those in Henry the Eighth's reign, more than half a century after the discovery of the American mines.

Stow sets down the price of an ox in 1531 at £1, 6s. 8d., or £2 of our money, and a sheep at 2s. 10d., equal at present to 4s. 3d.; which does not materially differ from the valuation in Wolsey's catalogue.

In the 23d of Henry the Eighth, upon the Bishop of London exhorting the inferior clergy to contribute

* Anderson's History of Commerce, vol. i. p. 284.

towards paying the £100,000 which they had granted
to the king, to exempt them from a *præmunire*, the
clergy reply, " that twenty nobles [equal to about £10
of our money] is but a bare living for a priest, and that
their poverty forced them to refuse;"* and yet this is
a great improvement on the " £5 per annum," which
Fleetwood tells us was a sufficient income for a bachelor
clergyman in 1439.   In 1533, a statute enacts that no
person shall take above one halfpenny for a pound of
beef or pork, nor above three farthings for mutton and
veal.†

These notices are far from being so full and satisfactory as could be wished, but such as they are, and in
the absence of countervailing evidence, they appear to
be inconsistent with the idea that prices had risen, at
least in any remarkable degree, after the discovery of
America, and prior to the great importations of silver
from the more abundant mines of Potosi.

Mexico was invaded in 1519, and the conquest of
Peru was achieved in 1539.   In 1545, the mines of
the Cerro de Potosi were discovered, and after that we
begin to hear complaints of the high price of provisions.

* Anderson's History of Commerce, vol. ii. p. 56.    † Ib.

But let us examine whether these complaints were really attributable, as has been supposed, to the greater plenty of the metals, or to the adulterations and debasements of the coin which disgraced the reigns of Henry VIII. and his son,—a series of the most shameless frauds perhaps ever perpetrated in any age or country.

I propose to take up this subject, with notices of the range of prices from 1545 to 1574, in my next letter.

## LETTER XIII.

*American mines and European prices—Period from the
discovery of Potosi in 1545, to the general rise of prices
about 1574.*

THE Oxford tables of prices, for which we are indebted
to Mr Loyd, do not go farther back than 1583, and in
the absence of direct and conclusive documents, reference has frequently been made to works upon other
subjects, which contain incidental allusions to the advance of prices in those days—among others, to the
Sermons of Bishop Latimer, preached before King Edward VI. The first of these sermons, which was delivered
in the " Shroudes at Paule's Church in London, 17th
day of January 1548," is specially referred to by Mr
Jacob,* who cites the following passage in which Latimer alludes to his family history :—" My father was a

* History of the Precious Metals, vol. ii. pp. 77, 78.

yeoman, and had no landes of hys owne, only he had a
farme of three or four pounds by yeare at the uttermost,
and hereupon he tilled so muche as kept halfe a dossen
men.  He had walke for an hundred sheepe, and my
mother milked thirty kyne.  He was able and did find
the king a harnesse, and with himselfe and his horse
while he came to the place that he should receive the
king's wages.  I can remember that I buckled his
harnesse when he went into Blackheath field.  He
kept me to schole, or els I had not been able to have
preached before the king's maiestie now.  He married
my sisters with five pounds or twenty nobles a piece,
so that he brought them up in godliness and feare of
God.  He kept hospitality for his poor neighbours;
and some alms he gave to the poore; and all this did
he of the said farme.  Whene he that now hath it,
payeth sixteen pounds by the year, or more, and is not
able to do anything for hys prince, for himselfe, nor
for hys children, or give a cup of drink to the poore."

On this passage, Mr Jacob has the following com-
mentary:—" This rise of rents, which the bishop states
in a manner not remarkable for its precision, does,
however, deserve notice.  When his father rented the
farm in question (in Lincolnshire) at three or four

pounds a-year, may refer to the time of the battle of
Blackheath, fought in the reign of Henry VII., 1497,
or fifty years before the sermon was delivered, when
the same farm was rented at sixteen pounds or more.
This advance in rent, amounting to 400 or 500 per
cent., must, however, be in some measure apparent
rather than real; because in the interval great alterations had been made in the coin.   In the. reign of
Henry VII. the pound weight of silver was coined into
45s., twenty of which made £1 sterling.   In that part
of the reign of Edward VI. in which Latimer preached
—for before his death an improvement took place—the
coin had been deteriorated, and the pound of silver was
coined into 72s.   The pound of 1497 was worth 26s.
8d. in our present money, and the pound of 1548 no
more than 17s. 8d.; and consequently the advance of
rent from £4 to £16 nominally was really from £5, 6s.
8d. to £14, 2s., or little more than 160 per cent.   This
is a much more probable rate of advance than what
would be inferred from the bare words of the sermon."*

In this statement, Mr Jacob would seem to have
altogether mistaken the figures.   In the reign of Henry

* Jacob's History of the Precious Metals, vol. ii. pp. 78, 79.

VII., the pound weight of silver was coined, not into
45s., but into 37s. 6d.  In that part of the reign of
Edward VI. in which Latimer preached (1548), the
pound weight of silver was coined, not into 72s., but
into £6, 12s., of which sum £4, 4s. was retained as
seignorage.  The pound-sterling of 1497 was worth,
not 26s. 8d., but 31s., and the pound-sterling of 1548
was worth, not 17s. 8d., but 9s. 3¾d.*  Consequently
the advance of rent from £4 to £16 nominally, was
really from £6, 4s. to £7, 9s., or about 20 per cent.,
instead of the fancied advance of 160 per cent., which
Mr Jacob places to the credit of Potosi.  An advance
of 20 per cent. on the rent of a particular farm, at the
distance of fifty years, is, of course, no indication either
of a rise or fall of general prices.

"The bishop," adds Mr Jacob, "was evidently un-
aware that the influx of gold and silver from the new
world was producing a gradual increase of prices, and
like other persons in that age, sought, with more zeal
than judgment, to find the causes of this extraordinary
phenomenon.  He attributes this, which he treated as
a great evil, to enclosures, to sheep walks, to regraters,

* See Harris on Money and Coins, part ii. p. 2.—Silver here is
taken at 5s. 2d. an ounce, the mint price prior to 1816.

forestallers, and to any cause but the true one, which, in his warmth against his neighbours, he had totally overlooked, or was unacquainted with."

Latimer's judgment, I suspect, was not so much at fault as his commentator imagines, and his zeal was righteously directed against one of the most impudent frauds recorded in history. In 1497, the silver in the pound-sterling was equal to 31s. of our present money; in 1548, to only 9s. 3¾d.; and in 1551, by a still further adulteration and debasement, the silver coins were made little better than tokens or counters—the pound-sterling being worth only 4s. 7¾d.! To such length did the degradation go, that the mint value of silver was raised to one-half that of gold; one pound of gold and 2·011 lbs. of fine silver being actually coined into the same sum! A pound weight of silver which the year before had been coined into £7, 4s., was now coined into £14, 8s.! Latimer, though a court preacher, was not ignorant either of this fraud or of its consequences. Hear his amusing sarcasm, in a sermon delivered in March 1549, which appears to have escaped the notice of Mr Jacob:—"We have now," he says, "a pretty little shilling, indeed a very pretty one. I have but one I think in my purse, and the last day I had put it away almost for an old groat, and so I trust some will take them. The fineness of the silver I cannot see; but there is printed a fine sentence: *Timor Domini fons vitæ vel sapientiæ.*" In the next sermon, he says, "Thus they burdened me ever with sedition. And wot ye what? I chanced in my last sermon to speak a merry word of the new shilling to refresh my auditory, how I was like to put away my new shilling for an old groat. I was therein noted to speak seditiously. I have now gotten one fellowe more, a companion of sedition, and wot you who is my fellowe? *Esay* the prophet. I spake but of a little prettie shilling, but he speaketh to *Jerusalem* after another sort, and was so bold as to meddle with their coynes. Thou proud, thou haughty city of Jerusalem: *Argentum tuum versum est in scoriam—* thy silver is turned into, what? into testions? *scoriam,* into dross. Ah, seditious wretch! what had he to do with the mint? Why should he not have left that matter to some master of policy to reprove? thy silver is dross, it is not fine, it is counterfeit, thy silver it is turned; thou hadst good silver. What pertained that unto *Esay?* Marry he espied a piece of divinity in that policy, he threatneth them God's vengeance for it. He went to the root of the matter, which was covetousness; he espied two points in it, that either it came of covetousness, which became him to reprove: or else that it tended to the hurt of poore people; for the naughtiness of the silver was the occasion of dearth of all things in the realm. He imputeth it to them as a crime. He may be called a master of sedition indeed. Was not this a seditious fellow, to tell them this even to their faces?"*

I have cited at length these quaint passages, which may perhaps tend to relieve the very dry discussion which I am now pursuing; and I have done so for the purpose mainly of showing you, that the real cause of the apparent elevation of prices which occurred during the first half of the sixteenth century must be ascribed, as it was then universally ascribed, to profligate tamperings with the weight and purity of the coin, and not to additional supplies from the mines of the new world. Were silver now our exclusive standard, and an act of parliament passed to-morrow, ordering a threepenny piece to pass current for a shilling, prices would the following day rise fourfold. But this is exactly the same thing as ordering the quantity of fine silver contained in a threepenny piece to be mixed with baser metal and coined into a shilling. The size of the coin is

---

* Cited by Harris, part ii. p. 8.

nothing—the alloy is nothing—the value resides exclusively in the quantity of the precious metal which the
coin contains.  Creditors, annuitants, mortgagees, landowners, every class of the community except debtors,
would be defrauded, all contracts for money would
thereby be evaded, but nominal prices would be raised;
and land, now let for £4, would let for £16, just as it
did in Bishop Latimer's day.  I surely need not add,
that the landlord would be no gainer by the fraud, as
his £16 would, after the perpetration of so disgraceful
an imposition, bring him no more of any thing than his
£4 did before—his four threepenny pieces, call them what
you might, would just purchase what he could formerly
have bought for a shilling.

Before the end of 1551 these abuses were corrected,
and the coins were raised to more than four times the
value of the debased money of the same denomination.
The standard then adopted comes so very near that
which was afterwards permanently established in the
43d of Elizabeth, that it will not be necessary to fa-
tigue you during the remainder of this inquiry by noting
the difference between the former and present value of
money.

Of the twenty-nine years which elapsed between the

discovery of Potosi and the general enhancement of prices in Europe, unfortunately the prices of only eleven are preserved by Bishop Fleetwood, and it is very remarkable, that in no fewer than ten of these the price of wheat is set down at 8s. a-quarter. Fleetwood explains that the price did not remain fixed exactly at this sum, but that the variations were so inconsiderable, that landlords, in settling their rents with the farmers, agreed to estimate it at this price for these years. If Fleetwood's object, however, was, as it appears to have been, to give only years of more than usually high or low prices, we may presume, from his silence, that no general enhancement took place in the money value of corn. The average of the eleven years referred to is 8s. 10½d.

In 1548, according to Strype's Eccles. Memorials, wheat was 6s. 8d. per quarter; barley, malt, and rye, 5s.; pease and beans, 4s.; but, owing to the shamefully debased state of the coins, we can make no correct computation of the modern value of these sums.

In 1553 (1st and 2d Philip and Mary), an act was passed, enacting " that when the common price of wheat shall not exceed 6s. 8d. per quarter, rye 4s., and barley 3s. per quarter, then these three kinds of corn may be

exported anywhere but to the king and queen's ene-
mies."* From this we may infer, that these rates were
accounted ordinary or average, or at least fair and moderate prices. The actual price of wheat in 1553, as we
learn from the Chronicon Preciosum, was 8s. per quarter.

In 1554, Queen Mary grants twenty marks, or £13,
6s. 8d., annually for the competent exhibition and support of a student of law.†

The price of a good sheep, in 1557, is set down by
Fleetwood at 2s. 10d.; which is less than in Wolsey's
catalogue in 1530, and less than in Edward the Second's
tariff in 1315.‡

In 1559, Queen Elizabeth gave her physician in
ordinary a salary of £100 a-year; but the salaries of
professors in both universities continued at £40, the
sum settled by Henry VIII.§

About 1563, I think, we first begin to perceive some
faint indications of the general and sustained rise of
prices which was approaching; for by an ordinance of
that year (5th of Elizabeth) exportation is allowed when
wheat reaches 10s. a-quarter; rye, pease, and beans, 8s.;
malt, 6s. 8d. We may hence infer, that these had now

* Anderson's History of Commerce, vol. ii. p. 96.
† Ib. p. 97.        ‡ Ib. p. 103.        § Ib. p. 106.

come to be considered ordinary or moderate prices.   In the same year, in a treaty between England and Scotland for the punishment of robberies on the borders, the following prices of cattle and sheep are settled, viz. :—

An ox above four years old,   .   .   .   40s. sterling.

Every cow, . . . . . . . . . 30s.   „

Every ox above two years old,   .   .   30s.   „

Every old sheep, . · . . . . . .   6s.   „

Every hog (or young sheep),   .   .   .   3s.   „

These prices, allowing for the difference in the coins, exceed slightly those formerly noticed.*

In 1663, the first statute for the relief of the poor was enacted; and another act, passed for regulating the hiring, &c. of servants, states, "That the wages ascertained in former acts were now become insufficient by reason of the advanced prices of all necessaries since those times."† This seems to afford undeniable evidence that that progressive elevation of general prices had now begun, which appears so apparent ten years afterwards, and the causes of which I shall next proceed to examine.

The average annual supply of the precious metals

* Anderson's History of Commerce, vol. ii. pp. 117, 118.

† Ib. vol. ii. p. 119.

during the period we have been examining is computed by Humboldt[*] to have been £2,291,666, which, for the twenty-eight years ending with 1573, gives a total of £64,166,548,—a sum nearly equal to the original stock before the discovery of America as estimated by Jacob, with the addition of all the quantities imported after the discovery and prior to 1545.

I trust that I have thus far established the propositions with which I set out,[†] by proving,

1st, That "during the period which immediately succeeded the discovery of the American mines, a considerable addition was made to the stock of the precious metals which had previously circulated in the commercial world, but that this addition was accompanied with little or no augmentation of general prices in England;" and,

2d, That "during the period which intervened between the discovery of Potosi and the great reduction which took place in the cost of producing silver, during which interval still greater additions were annually made to the stock of the precious metals, no marked or sensible rise of general prices took place."

* Essai Politique, liv. iv. chap. xi.
† *Ante*, Letter X.

## LETTER XIV.

*American mines and European prices—Period from 1574 to 1650, when the first enhancement of prices consequent upon the discovery appears to have ceased.*

WE have now arrived at a period when general prices reached a much higher level, which they have maintained (although of course with many fluctuations) ever since.

The average price of wheat, as we have seen, was (in money of our time),

| | | |
|---|---|---|
| From 1339 to 1416, . . . . | £1 5 | $9\frac{1}{3}$ |
| „ 1423 „ 1451, . . . . | 1 1 | $3\frac{1}{3}$ |
| „ 1453 „ 1492, . . . . | 0 14 | 1 |
| „ 1494 „ 1545, . . . . | 0 14 | 5 |
| „ 1551 „ 1562, . . . . | 0 8 | $10\frac{1}{2}$ |

For 1575, and four preceding years, in which the

prices of wheat are noticed,* the average appears to
have been    .    .    .    .    .    £1   2   2
In 1583 the price was    .    .    .        0  17   2

After this we have the prices of every year given;
and dividing the remainder of the period into decades,
the averages were,

From 1584 to 1593 (inclusive),  .   .   £1   1   3½
   „  1594 „ 1603      „      .   .    1  14   2
   „  1604 „ 1613      „      .   .    1   9   9
   „  1614 „ 1623      „      .   .    1  14  10½
   „  1624 „ 1633      „      .   .    1  18  10¼
   „  1634 „ 1643      „      .   .    2   0   5½
   „  1644 „ 1653      „      .   .    2   6   4¼

Concurrently with this great enhancement of prices
in Europe, the average annual supply of the precious
metals (taking Humboldt's estimate†) was, from 1545
to 1600, £2,291,666, which, for the twenty-seven years
ending with 1600, gives    .    .    .    £61,874,982

From 1600 to 1700 the annual supply
is estimated at £3,333,333, which, for the
remaining fifty-three years of the period
under consideration, gives    .    .    .    £176,666,649

Together,    £238,541,631

* See Malthus' Principles of Political Economy, 2d edit. p. 241.
† Essai Politique, liv. iv. chap. xi.

Now we have seen that in the two previous periods which we have had under review (viz. the periods from 1492 to 1545, and from 1545 to 1573), the increased supplies of the precious metals did *not* produce a general elevation of prices. Here we have a still farther increase, which *is* followed by such elevation. In the previous periods we had the same antecedents, but without this consequence. If the enhancement of prices during this last period was specifically the effect of the additional supplies, why was a similar effect, to some extent at least, not perceptible before? Like causes should produce like effects. If the prices of grain were tripled in consequence of the supply of silver being increased threefold, why were they not doubled when the supply of silver was doubled? Is there not some reason to doubt, then, whether these phenomena stand in the relation of cause and effect? and is it not worth while to inquire whether they are not both of them collateral effects proceeding from a cause common to both—namely, a change in the cost of production, an altered relation of the metals to the labour and capital by which they were produced—a cause, as we have seen in the case of other commodities, quite adequate to produce the effect, quite sufficient to account for an alteration of relative value, independently of any change in the actual relative quantities of the metals upon the whole, and commodities upon the whole?

In pursuing this inquiry, we must now turn our attention for a little from Europe and European prices to America, and the mining operations which were carried on there during the period of which we have been speaking.

Till 1525, Europe received little silver from America. The importations were chiefly of such gold as the first invaders could obtain by persuasion or violence from the natives, who appear to have valued it very little. After the conquest of Mexico and Peru, silver-mining was begun in earnest; and the quantity of that metal imported into Europe exceeded the importations of gold in the proportion of 60 to 1. Silver was then the standard of money in every country of Europe.

That metal, as I have already said, is seldom found, in large quantities at least, in its native state, but is usually combined in small proportions with other mineral substances. The Cerro de Potosi is said originally to have yielded 50 per cent. of fine silver, or half the ore in weight. But the richness of the ores diminished as the works increased in depth.

Humboldt informs us, that from 1574 to 1789 the mean richness of these ores diminished in the proportion of 170 to 1. The average amount of silver extracted in Mexico from a quintal (100 lbs.) of the ore is said to be from three to four ounces. The various kinds and qualities of the ores, and the operations and processes which are necessary to bring the ore to the surface, and afterwards to separate the silver from it, are minutely stated by Humboldt in his admirable Political Essay on New Spain,* to which I must refer you, as it would be beyond my design to enter into such details in this place: a certain amount of explanation, however, is necessary.

From 1545 to 1571 the ores of Potosi were all smelted. This process is thus described: Portable furnaces were erected on the mountains which surround the town of Potosi, wherever the wind blew with impetuosity. These furnaces were cylindrical tubes of clay, very broad, and pierced with a great number of holes. The Indians threw in layers of silver ore, galena, and charcoal; and the current of air which entered at the holes into the interior of the furnace quickened the

* Book iv. chap. xi.

flame, and gave it great intensity. If the wind blew too strong, and too much fuel was consumed, the furnaces were removed to a lower situation. The argentiferous masses thus obtained were resmelted in the cottages of the Indians. The fire was blown by ten or twelve persons at once, through copper tubes a yard or two in length, and pierced at the lower extremity with a very small hole; but a large quantity of silver always remained in the *scoriæ* without combining with the lead.\*

Such were the rude methods by which the first supplies of silver that reached the European markets were obtained; but a great improvement was about to be effected, which very much increased the quantity of silver, and diminished to a corresponding extent the cost of procuring it.

" The amalgamation of silver ores, and the ingenious process now used in the new world, to which we owe the greater part of the valuable metals existing in Europe, or which have flowed from Europe to Asia, goes no farther back than the year 1557. It was invented in Mexico by a miner of Pachuca, of the name of Bar-

\* Essai Politique, liv. iv. chap. xi.

tholome de Medina. From the documents preserved in the archives of the *despacho general de Indias,* and from the researches of Don Juan Diaz de la Calle, there cannot remain a doubt of the true author of the invention, which has sometimes been attributed to the Canon Henrique Garces, who, in 1566, began to work the mercury mines of Huancavelica, and sometimes to Fernandez de Velasco, who, in 1571, introduced the Mexican amalgamation into Peru. It is not so certain, however, that Medina, who was born in Europe, had not already made experiments in amalgamation before coming to Pachuca. Cold amalgamation was found so profitable in Mexico, that in 1562, five years after the first discovery of the process of Medina, there were already thirty-five works at Zacatecas, in which minerals were treated with mercury."*

It is impossible to overrate the importance of this discovery to mining industry, but it is not easy to ascertain exactly to what extent it reduced the expense of producing silver. The reduction, however, must have been very great. Humboldt says, that the proportion of silver extracted from the ores by mercury was in the

* Humboldt's Political Essay on New Spain (Black's Translation), vol. iii. p. 253.

proportion of $3\frac{1}{2}$ to 1 of that produced by smelting.*
The supply of silver, in fact, varies directly as the supply of mercury, and its value is as much dependent on
the price of mercury as the value of iron is dependent
on the cost of fuel. " The quantity of silver," says
Humboldt, "does not so much depend upon the abundance and intrinsic richness of the ores, as on the
facility with which the miners procure the mercury
necessary for amalgamation." †

There are very few mines of quicksilver in the world.
America after this invention was very insufficiently supplied, and at a great cost, chiefly from Almaden in Spain.

At length, in 1567, was discovered the famous quicksilver mine of Huancavelica in Peru,‡ the cinnabar

* Humboldt's Political Essay on New Spain, vol. iii. p. 250.
† Ib. vol. iii. p. 375.
‡ From this mine, between 1570 and 1645, there were ex-
tracted the following quantities of mercury :—

| | | | | |
|---|---|---|---|---|
| From 1570 to 1576, | . | . | . | 9,137 quintals. |
| „ 1576 „ 1586, | . | . | . | 60,000 „ |
| „ 1586 „ 1589, | . | . | . | 31,500 „ |
| „ 1590 „ 1598, | . | . | . | 59,850 „ |
| „ 1599 „ 1603, | . | . | . | 20,000 „ |
| „ 1604 „ 1610, | . | . | . | 19,000 „ |
| „ 1611 „ 1615, | . | . | . | 30,000 ;, |
| „ 1616 „ 1622, | . | . | . | 59,463 „ |
| „ 1623 „ 1645, | . | . | . | 96,600 „ |

of which had long before been used by the Incas for painting themselves. The working of this mine by the crown of Spain was not begun till the month of September 1570, the year before Fernandez de Velasco introduced the Mexican amalgamation process into Peru.* The miners of the new world were thus supplied with abundance of the material which of all others was most necessary to enable them to carry on their operations.

Velasco, having proposed to the viceroy of Peru to introduce the process of amalgamation into Potosi, he succeeded in the attempt in 1571; and of the mercury produced by the mine of Huancavelica towards the end of the sixteenth century, more than from 6000 to 7000 quintals were consumed in the works of Potosi.† The ores which during the first years had been thrown aside as too poor to be smelted in the portable furnaces, were now wrought to advantage. Even old barrows were searched for the ores which had formerly been rejected as useless, but were now subjected to the new process.

Now, mark well the *dates* of these discoveries and improvements, and turn once more to the prices of grain

* Humboldt's Political Essay on New Spain, vol. iii. p. 310.
† Ib. vol. iii. p. 377.

in England. From 1545 to 1571, we have the silver extracted from the ores by smelting, and we see that only the richer ores could be made available by fusion, while the mean richness of the American ores did not exceed three or four ounces of silver to the quintal. In 1554 (1st and 2d Philip and Mary, c. 5), corn is forbidden to be exported except when the price of wheat did not exceed 6s. 8d., rye 4s., and barley 3s. per quarter —the coin being almost of our present standard.

In 1557, a Mexican miner discovers the method of treating silver ores with mercury. In 1558 (1st Elizabeth, c. 11), wheat rises to 23s. a-quarter, but grain may still be exported when the price of wheat is not above 6s. 8d., rye 4s., and barley 3s. a-quarter. These last prices appear still to be considered a fair medium for both producers and consumers.

In 1562, we find thirty-five mines at work in Mexico, where " cold amalgamation " was practised. In 1563 (5th Elizabeth), grain may be exported when the price of wheat did not exceed 10s., rye, pease, and beans, 8s., and malt 6s. 8d. a-quarter. These were therefore now considered fair moderate prices, as 6s. 8d., 4s., and 3s. had been formerly.

In 1570, the great quicksilver mine of Huancavelica

in South America, begins to be worked, and in 1571 the process of amalgamation is introduced into Peru, and the ores of Potosi subjected to it.

In 1573 (8th Elizabeth), " about Lammas, wheat was sold in London at 3s. 3d. the bushel, but shortly after it was raised to 4s. 4d., 5s. 6d., 6s. 6d., and 7s. 9d. [equal to 26s., 34s. 8d., 44s., 52s., and 62s. the quarter], which continued long after, yet *there was no want to him that wanted not money.*" * In 1574, wheat is quoted by Fleetwood at 40s. a-quarter—in 1587, at £3, 4s. The price of ordinary day labour in 1575 was 8d.

In 1586 and 1590, new methods of applying mercury to mining purposes were discovered,† and the "hot amalgamation" was introduced. In 1593 (35th Elizabeth, c. 7), wheat might be exported when not above 20s. a-quarter, that being now deemed a fair and reasonable price, as 10s. had been in 1563. This price in 1604 (1st James I., c. 25), is raised to 26s. 8d.; in 1623 (21st James I., c. 28), to 32s.; and in 1627 (3d Charles I., c. 4), the same rate is continued; while by

* A True Relation of the most remarkable Dearths and Famines, &c., 1748, cited by Mr Jacob—History of Precious Metals, vol. ii. p. 74.

† Humboldt's Political Essay on New Spain, vol. iii. pp. 252, 266.

Cromwell's ordinance (in 1656), the price is raised to 40s. a-quarter. In 1601, the price of ordinary day labour was 10d.; in 1651, it rose to 1s. 2d.* In short,

* That this elevation of prices was not confined to England, nor exclusively to grain, is proved by the following table of prices in France, extracted and abridged by Mr Jacob, from a publication by Coignard, at Paris, 1746, entitled "Essai sur les Monnois, ou Reflections sur le Rapport entre l'Argent et les Denrées:"—

| Year. | Article. | Price. | | | Year. | Price. | | |
|---|---|---|---|---|---|---|---|---|
| 1492, | Setier of wheat, | . . £0 | 15 | 0 | 1588, | £8 | 14 | 0 |
| „ | Grinding a setier, | . . 0 | 1 | 2 | 1587, | 0 | 5 | 10 |
| 1494, | A pigeon, . . . . . | 0 | 0 | 6 | 1588, | 0 | 7 | 2 |
| „ | A rabbit, . . . . . | 0 | 3 | 0 | „ | 0 | 17 | 0 |
| „ | A capon, . . . . . | 0 | 3 | 0 | „ | 0 | 17 | 0 |
| „ | A pig, . . . . . . | 0 | 6 | 0 | „ | 4 | 2 | 0 |
| „ | 100 herrings, | . . 0 | 16 | 8 | 1587, | 3 | 10 | 0 |
| 1495, | Setier of wheat, | . . 0 | 11 | 5 | „ | 6 | 5 | 0 |
| 1499, | Setier of wheat, | . . 1 | 6 | 8 | 1588, | 9 | 0 | 0 |
| 1500, | Setier of wheat, | . . 1 | 10 | 0 | 1573, | 14 | 15 | 0 |
| 1501, | Setier of wheat, | . . 1 | 10 | 0 | 1575, | 6 | 13 | 4 |
| „ | A capon, . . . . . | 0 | 3 | 0 | 1578, | 0 | 19 | 0 |
| 1502, | A pound of candles, | . 0 | 1 | 0 | 1587, | 0 | 7 | 6 |
| „ | A pint of wine, . . | • 0 | 0 | 4 | 1577, | 0 | 3 | 0 |
| „ | A pint of oil, | . . . 0 | 1 | 10 | „ | 0 | 11 | 0 |
| „ | A voie of firewood, | . 0 | 18 | 4 | 1575, | 4 | 15 | 0 |
| 1503, | A minot of charcoal, | . 0 | 1 | 7 | 1572, | 0 | 8 | 0 |
| „ | A pound of butter, | . 0 | 0 | 10 | 1578, | 0 | 5 | 6 |
| | | £8 | 10 | 4 | | £62 | 15 | 4 |

This rise of prices, which so much exceeds what took place in England in the same interval, was partly owing to the debasement of the silver coin in the intermediate period.

with every improvement in the working of the mines,
or, what is the same thing, with every reduction in the
cost of producing silver, the value of grain would appear
to have risen in England.

I have now, I trust, sufficiently established the third
proposition laid down in my tenth letter, namely,—that
during the 4th period—that which followed the general
adoption of the process of amalgamation—the continued
increase of the supply of silver (unlike what took place
in the two former periods) *was* accompanied by a great
and permanent rise of prices ; and hence that we have
very strong reason to conclude that the general elevation
of prices which then occurred was attributable to a cause
peculiar to this 4th period, namely—the diminished cost
of producing silver; and that the increase of quantity,
instead of being the efficient cause of the elevation of
prices, was simply a collateral effect.

## LETTER XV.

*American mines and European prices — Century from 1650 to 1750, when a second general elevation of prices took place.*

You will remember that my fourth proposition was, "that during the century which succeeded 1650, when, according to Baron Humboldt, prices appear to have reached the greatest elevation, still larger additions were made to the supply of silver than any which had preceded, *without* any material change in the cost of production, and that general prices did *not* exceed those of the immediately preceding period; and, *lastly*, that a second reduction of the cost of producing silver, which took place after the middle of the eighteenth century, was followed by a second enhancement of prices." This appears to me to complete the argument, and to render it positively certain that the rise of prices, in both instances, and their continuance at the higher level, are attributable, not to increased supply, but to diminished cost.

Still following the Oxford tables, and taking averages of ten years, the prices of wheat for a century after 1653 are the following, viz. :—

| | | | |
|---|---|---|---|
| From 1654 to 1663, | . . . . | £2 3 | 3¼ |
| „ 1664 „ 1673, | . . . . | 1 13 | 6¾ |
| „ 1674 „ 1683, | . . . . | 1 19 | 8¾ |
| „ 1684 „ 1693, | . . . . | 1 13 | 11 |
| „ 1694 „ 1703, | . . . . | 2 2 | 6 |
| „ 1704 „ 1713, | . . . . | 1 18 | 9¾ |
| „ 1714 „ 1723, | . . . . | 1 13 | 8 |
| „ 1724 „ 1733, | . . . . | 1 14 | 3¼ |
| „ 1734 „ 1743, | . . . . | 1 13 | 10½ |
| „ 1744 „ 1753, | . . . . | 1 9 | 9½ |

These prices, it will be seen, did not exceed the average prices of the period from 1563 to 1653; but the importations of the precious metals during the century under consideration were very much greater. Humboldt computes the additions to the precious metals,

from 1600 to 1700, at £3,333,333 per annum, which
for forty-seven years would amount to    £156,666,651
And from 1700 to 1750, at £4,687,500
   per annum, which, for fifty years,
   would give . . . . . .    234,375,000
And for the following three years, at
   £7,354,166 per annum, . . .    22,062,498

Amounting altogether to the enormous
   sum of . . . . . . .    £413,104,149

Yet it appears that general prices were not sensibly
affected by these unparalleled additions to the supply
of the precious metals.  Wages in 1601, we have seen,
were 10d. a-day; and Arthur Young* estimates the
average price of labour for the whole of the seventeenth
century at only 10½d.  The prices of wheat, as given
in the Windsor tables, he reduces to the following
average :—

For the 17th century, . £1 18  2 per quarter.
  „   18th century, .   1 18  7      „

being a rise of only 5d. a-quarter,† including in the

* Annals of Agriculture, No. 270, p. 88.
† Progressive Value of Money, p. 75.

average the higher prices which distinguished the latter
half of the eighteenth century, to which I shall immediately advert.  There seems, therefore, no reason
to conclude that the large and continued importation of
silver produced any effect upon prices after the great
and marked rise in the end of the sixteenth century,
which, as already seen, was consequent on the reduced
cost of production.

Writing in 1778, Hume remarks, that " there seem
to have been two periods in which prices rose remarkably in England—namely, that in Queen Elizabeth's
reign, where they are computed to have doubled, and
that in the present age.  Between the two," he adds,
" there seems to have been a stagnation."*  The reason
he gives for it is, " that industry during the intermediate
period would appear to have increased as fast as gold
and silver, and kept commodities nearly at a par with
money."†  The fact stated by Hume is unquestionable;
but the reason he gives for it would seem to be founded
on pure assumption.  How does it appear that industry
kept more upon a par with silver from the reign of
Elizabeth to that of George III., than it did from the

* Hume's History of England, App. iii.    † Ib.

reign of Henry VII. to that of Elizabeth? and why should silver be different in this respect from every other commodity?   As far as its value is concerned, why should it be different from iron and other metals, the permanent value of which, let their supply in proportion to industry be what it will, rises and falls with the cost of their production?  You find iron at one period at £6 a-ton, at another at £2, at a third remaining at a uniform price?   Would it be held a sufficient reason for this to say, that during the intermediate period silver and gold would appear to have increased as fast as iron, and kept its value nearly at a par with money? Surely it would not.  Were it clearly shown that the fall from £6 to £2 was consequent on a reduction of the cost of producing iron, the natural inference regarding the intermediate period would be, that during that period the cost had remained the same.

But it may be said that the rise of prices in England depended not upon the quantities of bullion imported into Europe from the American mines, but upon the proportion which was actually converted into money in our own country.   Now what were the quantities coined?

The coinage of England from 1599 to 1619 amounted
to . . . . . . . £4,779,314*

From 1619 to 1638 it amounted to      6,900,042

From 1638 to 1657 to . . .      7,733,521†
_____

In all, to  £19,312,877

Hume states, on the authority of Dr
Davenant, who had examined the re-
gisters of the mint, that the whole
coinage between 1558 and 1659 was      19,832,476
_____

Thus leaving for the period between
1558 and 1599 only . . .      £519,599
_____

If the problem cannot be solved by a reference to
importations of bullion, these figures, which indicate the
amount of bullion converted into coin in England, will
certainly not help us to a solution. If, in consequence
of a coinage of little more than half a million, from 1558
to 1599, prices in England were tripled, why should
they have remained comparatively stationary from 1599
to 1657 with a coinage of more than nineteen millions?

* Hume's History of England, App. to reign of James I.
† Ib. chap. lxii.

In short, look at this subject in whatever light,—regard it from whatever point of view you will,—we are constantly thrown back upon *cost of production*, as the regulator of value and the arbiter of price.

## LETTER XVI.

*American mines and European prices—Period from* 1750
*to the suspension of cash payments in* 1797.

AT length—after the long interval of more than 100
years, during which prices had remained almost stationary, notwithstanding the unprecedented additions that
were made to the metallic wealth of Europe—after the
middle of the eighteenth century, we witness another
permanent and general enhancement, only less striking
than that which occurred towards the end of the sixteenth century. The great rise which had taken place
in the price of grain and other provisions, just before
the publication of the Wealth of Nations in 1776, is
noticed by Adam Smith, who imputes it, however,
rather to a tract of bad seasons which had then occurred than to a fall in the value of the precious metals.
" As to the price of corn itself," he says, " it has during

the sixty-four first years of the present century, and before the late extraordinary course of bad seasons, been somewhat lower than it was during the sixty-four years of the preceding century.  This fact is attested not only by the accounts of Windsor market, but by the public fiars of all the different counties of Scotland, and by the accounts of several different markets in France, which have been collected with great diligence and fidelity by M. Messance and M. Dupre de St Maur.  The evidence is more complete than could well have been expected in a matter which is naturally so very difficult to be ascertained.  As to *the high price of corn during these last ten or twelve years*, it can be sufficiently accounted for from the badness of the seasons, without supposing any degradation in the value of silver.  The opinion, therefore, that silver is continually sinking in value, seems not to be founded upon any good observations, either upon the prices of corn or upon those of other provisions."*

What appears to have misled this acute observer, in reference to the phenomena then passing under his own immediate observation, was, that "the rise in the price

* Wealth of Nations, book i. chap. xi.

of provisions, which had been the subject of so much reasoning and conversation, did not affect all sorts of provisions equally."* Now, *theoretically*, there can be no doubt that "any rise in the money price of goods, which proceeds altogether from the degradation of the value of silver [or the metal constituting the standard], will affect all sorts of goods equally, and raise their price universally;"† but then it will only do so, *other things remaining the same.* If the cost of producing the goods is diminished at the same time, and in the same proportion that the cost of producing the precious metals is diminished, no effect will be produced on the price of such goods. If again the cost of production in some departments is diminished, while in others it remains stationary, or is enhanced, a degradation of silver will in the one case have little or no effect, while in the other, prices will be increased or diminished. *Practically*, during a fall in the value of the precious metals, *other things generally do not remain the same;* cost of production in some departments is falling, in others rising, in others stationary; and hence we never actually see a simultaneous rise or fall in the value of *all*

* Wealth of Nations (M'Culloch's Edition), vol. i. p. 394.
† Ib.

things.  This, however, instead of invalidating rather strengthens and fortifies the doctrine of Smith, that a change in the real value of the precious metals raises or depresses the prices of all goods equally and universally when the cost of producing the goods themselves remains the same.  A change in the value of the precious metals acts upon the prices of all commodities; but in some instances its action is to a greater or less extent countervailed by causes operating in an opposite direction; and in these instances, therefore, the rise or fall of price may not be *apparent*.

Viewing from a greater distance the phenomena which began to manifest themselves to Adam Smith's observation, we are enabled to take a larger and more comprehensive survey of their causes.  The researches, too, of the great philosophic traveller, Humboldt, have subsequently thrown a flood of light upon this important, interesting, and difficult subject; and we can now pronounce with certainty that the extraordinary enhancement of general prices which occurred after the middle of the last century, and which was so sensibly felt in this country towards the conclusion of the American war, was caused by a diminution of the value of the metals.

First of all, let us contrast the prices of the first with those of the last half of the eighteenth century, taking the Oxford tables for our guide, and reducing the prices to averages of ten years as before. As already seen, the mean prices of the quarter of wheat were,

| | | | | |
|---|---|---|---|---|
| From 1704 to 1713, | . | . | . | £1 18 9¾ |
| „ 1714 „ 1723, | . | . | . | 1 13 8 |
| „ 1724 „ 1733, | . | . | . | 1 14 3¼ |
| „ 1734 „ 1743, | . | . | . | 1 13 10½ |
| „ 1744 „ 1753, | . | . | . | 1 9 9½ |

During the last half of the century the mean prices were,

| | | | | |
|---|---|---|---|---|
| From 1754 to 1763, | . | . | . | £1 15 8½ |
| „ 1764 „ 1773, | . | . | . | 2 10 6¾ |
| „ 1774 „ 1783, | . | . | . | 2 9 7¾ |

And from 1784 to 1797 (the year of the suspension of cash payments), . £2 16 3¾

| | | | | |
|---|---|---|---|---|
| The general average of the whole century was | . . . . | . | . | £2 1 1½ |
| The average of the first half, | . | . | | 1 13 8¼ |
| That of the last half, | . | . | . | 2 8 6¾ |

Contrasting the thirty years ending 1695 with the thirty years ending 1795, Mr Jacob computes the advance of prices during the latter period to have been from £1, 18s. 8d. to £2, 10s. 3d., or about 30 per cent.*

Nor was this rise confined to England. In Spain, the mean price of wheat in the market of Seville, from 1711 to 1726, was 14 reals 31 maravedis the fanega; from 1727 to 1752 it was 17 reals 22 maravedis; while from 1765 to 1787 it was 26 reals 11 maravedis.† At Dantzic, the average price of wheat, from 1700 to 1725, was 135 florins per last of 10 quarters; from 1775 to 1800 it was 337 florins per last, thus exhibiting an advance of nearly 150 per cent. over the prices of the earlier period.‡

And the advance was not on the price of corn alone. Mr Jacob gives an abstract of the prices of provisions furnished to Chelsea Hospital for the three years ending 1732, and the three years ending 1793, from which it appears that the advance on bread, beef, mutton, cheese, and butter, had been 20 per cent., and on pease, oatmeal, and coals, still more.§

* Jacob's History of the Precious Metals, vol. ii. p. 216.

† Ib. p. 207.    ‡ Ib. pp. 218, 219.

§ Ib. p. 219.—Consult also the account of the contract prices of articles of provision, &c., at Greenwich Hospital, given by Mr M'Culloch in his valuable Dictionary of Commerce (pp. 1060-61), and you will find evidence of the same general elevation

The price of ordinary labour rose to a corresponding extent. The mean price of common day labour during the eighteenth century is computed by Arthur Young to have been 10½d. In 1725, the Manchester justices settled wages at 1s. a-day for the best agricultural labourers from the middle of March to the middle of September—for common labourers, 10d. ; while from 1766 to 1770 Arthur Young estimates the wages of common day labour at 7s. 4½d. a-week (over the year), or 1s. 2½d. a-day nearly.*

The rise which took place in the price of provisions must have affected materially the comforts of the la-

of prices during the last half of the eighteenth century. The price of meat, which in 1750 was £1, 6s. 6d. per cwt., rose in 1775 to £1, 13s. 5d., and in 1795 to £2, 2s. 10d. ; the price of butter, which in 1750 was 5⅛d. a lb., rose in 1775 to 6¾d., and in 1795 to 8¼d. ; the price of cheese, which in 1750 was 3¼d. a lb., rose in 1795 to 5¼d. ; the price of pease, which in 1750 was 3s. 6d. a bushel, rose in 1775 to 7s. 6d., and in 1795 to 9s. 6d. ; oatmeal, from 4s. a bushel in 1750 to 5s. 3d. in 1775, and 6s. 4¾d. in 1795 —and other provisions in proportion ; while the wages of joiners rose from 2s. 8d. per day in 1750 to 2s. 10d. in 1795 ; of brick-layers, from 2s. 6d. to 3s. ; of masons, from 2s. 8d. to 2s. 10d. ; of plumbers, from 2s. 6d. to 3s. 3d. ; shoes, from 3s. 9d. to 4s. a pair ; coals, from £1, 7s. 7½d. to £1, 19s. 9d. a chaldron.

* See Malthus' Political Economy, 2d edit., p. 250.

bouring classes, for we find that in 1775, the poor rates, which before 1750 had not exceeded £730,000, now rose to a million and a half—that is, were more than doubled in fifteen years.*

* Porter's Progress of the Nation, p. 86 (edition 1847).

# LETTER XVII.

*American mines and European prices—State of the
mines after* 1750.

Now what were the causes of the marked and universal
enhancement of prices in Europe after the middle of
the eighteenth century, which I noticed in my last
letter? For an explanation of it, we must turn again
to the new world, and the work of Humboldt.

The average annual supply, which from 1700 to 1750
had been £4,687,500, or for fifty years, £234,375,000
increased from 1750 to 1800 to £7,354,166,

or for fifty years, . . . . . 367,708,300
_____

Difference between the first and last half
of the eighteenth century, . . . £133,333,300

This was undoubtedly a very great enlargement of
supply, but it will not account for the rise of prices; for
we have seen that at a former period, an addition of
more than 31 per cent. to the annual supply of the

metals produced no such effect, and at another that prices remained stationary, notwithstanding the supply was enlarged by upwards of 40 per cent. It would be contrary to every principle of just reasoning and legitimate induction, therefore, to conclude that in this instance the addition of nearly 57 per cent. to the then existing supply of the precious metals, was the cause of the great elevation of prices which occurred during the period we are now considering.

Again, we have seen at a former period, that the general enhancement of prices was due to the diminished cost of producing silver as its proper cause. Let us examine, then, whether a similar diminution of cost did not now, after an interval of more than 100 years, again occur, to which both the enlargement of the supply of silver, and the enhancement of prices, which manifested themselves after the middle of the eighteenth century, may be traced as collateral effects.

From 1750 to 1803, large quantities of gold were imported—a metal, as we shall afterwards see, produced under different conditions from silver. The produce of the Brazilian gold mines alone is computed during that period to have amounted to $1\frac{3}{4}$ millions sterling per annum, and the cost of producing silver was at the same time very much reduced. "When the price of mercury," says Humboldt, "has progressively lowered, the working of the mines has gone on increasing. In 1590, under the Viceroy Don Luis de Velasco II., a quintal of mercury was sold in Mexico for 187 piastres. But in the eighteenth century, the value of this metal had diminished to such a degree, that in 1750, the court distributed it to the miners at 82 piastres. Between 1767 and 1776 its price was 62 piastres the quintal. In 1777, under the administration of the minister Galvez, a royal decree fixed the price of the mercury of Almaden at 41 piastres, 2 reals, and that of Germany at 63 piastres." "From 1762 to 1781 the amalgamation works of New Spain destroyed the enormous quantity of 191,405 quintals, of which the value in America amounted to more than 60 millions of livres tournois," equal to £2,400,000 sterling.*

* Humboldt's Political Essay on New Spain, vol. iii. pp. 282, 83.
Humboldt gives the following table as proving the influence which the price of mercury exercises upon its consumption :—

| Periods. | Price per quintal. | Total Consumption. |
|---|---|---|
| 1762 to 1766, . . | 82 piastres. | 35,750 quintals. |
| 1767 ,, 1771, . . | 62 ,, | 42,000 ,, |
| 1772 ,, 1777, . . | 62 ,, | 53,000 ,, |
| 1778 ,, 1782, . . | 41 ,, | 59,000 ,, |

—New Spain, vol. iii. p. 285.

This great reduction in the cost of the principal and most expensive material used in mining processes, not only diminished the value of silver in relation to commodities, but stimulated the production, and greatly enlarged the supply of that metal. " The great mine of Valenciana, which during forty years yielded to its proprietors a clear profit of from £85,000 to £125,000 sterling yearly, had been neglected till the year 1760, and after ten years labour and expenditure, when the rich part of the vein had been reached, continued for upwards of forty years to yield more than half a million sterling in gold and silver. The rich district of Guanaxuato, which in the years before 1766 yielded only 380,000 ounces of silver yearly, produced in the latter years of its prosperity more than 1,500,000 ounces. The mineral repository of Catorce was only discovered in the year 1773, but it yielded a very large quantity both of gold and silver till 1798, when the value of the minerals declined. The vein of Biscaina, though it began to be worked at the beginning of the sixteenth century, did not become enormously productive till 1762, though in twelve years from that period the owner of it had gained a profit of more than a million sterling, with part of which he presented to the King of Spain two ships of war, one of them of one hundred and twenty guns; and, besides, lent him upwards of two hundred thousand pounds, which was never after repaid. The mines of the district of Zaccatecas were, about the year 1750, in such a state of abandonment, that they scarcely furnished silver to the amount of more than £100,000; but by the spirited exertions of an individual, Laborde, in a few years after their produce was raised to ten times that amount."* Such were the striking effects produced by the cheaper and more abundant supplies of mercury at once upon the produce of the precious metals, and the prices of commodities circulated by their means.

You will now understand the reason why the increased supplies of the metals during the last half of the eighteenth century acted upon prices, while those of the previous period created no such action. In the former case, more was produced, but produced with a less proportionate expenditure of labour and capital— in the latter, more was produced, but the additional production was unaccompanied with any diminution of cost. Hence, in the one case, a determinate quantity of

* Jacob's History of the Precious Metals, vol. ii. pp.152-3.

every commodity came to be exchanged for a greater
quantity of silver, because the same amount of labour
or capital which produced the commodity, would, if
employed in mining, have produced a greater quantity
of silver, and, in the other case, to be exchanged for
no more silver than before, because an equal amount
of labour or capital would have produced no more than
the former quantity of silver, and no more than the
former quantity of the other commodities to be exchanged by means of silver.

This rapid and in many respects superficial and
imperfect review of prices during the 300 years which
succeeded the discovery of the American mines, will
have fully answered the design I had in view, if it has
served to convince you, that cost of production alone is
the ultimate and permanent regulator of the relative
value of the materials of money, and consequently of
the value of money itself; and that the reason why the
mass of silver dug from the rich deposits of the new
world did not produce any marked effect on general
prices for seventy or eighty years after the discovery,
was, that seventy or eighty years elapsed before the
invention, at least before the practical introduction of
the cheaper and more efficacious method of extracting

the metal from its ores, and preparing it for the purposes of commerce.

Whether like causes, or any causes, exist to retard the effect of the recent marvellous discoveries of gold upon the money value of labour and commodities, is a question of pressing practical concernment, the importance of which to all classes of society it is quite impossible to overrate; and this question I propose to discuss in my next two letters.

# LETTER XVIII.

*Gold—conditions of its production as compared with silver
— California and Australia — recent accounts — remarkable rise in the price of labour and commodities
since the discovery of the gold-fields.*

THE progress of gold mining depends less than that
of silver upon the abundance of materials, such as
quicksilver, and the application to mining of large capitals, and improved mechanical and chemical processes.
Gold is more the product of direct and immediate labour
than silver. It is generally found either in its pure
state, or in combination only with other metals. When
traced to its matrix, it is discovered for the most part
in veins of quartz, and occurs in the shape of threads,
scales, or lumps; but in such small portions, compared
with the quantity of the rock through which it is dis-
seminated, that the expense of working quartz veins is

usually altogether disproportioned to the quantity of matrix gold which is obtained.

Deep mining, too, does not increase the return. Veins of other metals, when followed downwards, become in many cases more productive. Not so with gold; the deeper you go, the metal becomes proportionally less abundant, and frequently it disappears altogether.* Hence quartz mining has almost never been found a profitable enterprise. Nature, and time, and the seasons, do more in supplying us with gold than science and machinery. By the action of natural causes, the hard rocks which contain gold are disintegrated, the tops and surfaces of hills are loosened and ground down, and from the debris, the sand, gravel, and rubbish, washed by rain and torrents into the valleys below, we procure more abundant supplies of gold, in proportion to the labour employed, than can be forced from the parent rock by subjecting it to stamps, grinders, and crushing-mills. From the days of Job downwards, gold has been obtained chiefly by washing alluvial soils. " Surely there is a *vein for the silver*, and a place for gold where they fine it; as for the earth, out of it

---

* See a very able article, entitled Siberia and California, by Sir R. Murchison, in Quarterly Review for September 1850.

cometh bread; the stones of it are the place of sapphires, and *it hath dust of gold.*"

Where the working of matrix gold from quartz veins is carried on, complicated and expensive machinery is necessary; and where gold is found alloyed with other metals, as silver, copper, and iron, amalgamation, cupellation, fusion with lead, or other metallurgical processes, are resorted to. But a large proportion, perhaps nine-tenths of the gold of commerce, is obtained in a state of great purity, simply by digging and washing, —amalgamation with quicksilver being also used when the gold occurs mixed up in very minute portions with other substances.

In the Ural districts and Siberia, whence we now obtain a supply of about four millions a-year, the gold is obtained chiefly, if not altogether, from alluvial deposits. The mines of Gongo Soco and others in Brazil are worked in veins, but not profitably, by far the greater portion of the gold of South America being obtained, like that of Russia, from sands and auriferous alluvia. In California, hitherto, the case has been the same, although expensive preparations have lately been made for quartz mining on a large scale, which it is hoped may be successful. Our Australian diggings,

which have been worked since May 1851, form no
exception to the rule.  In creeks and valleys, in the
deserted channels of rivers, in the beds of existing
streams, in sand, gravel, or clay, in crevices of rocks,
the glittering treasure is discovered, sometimes in grains
and scales, and sometimes in lumps; and in some instances insulated masses have been found of a magnitude
till now unheard of.*   In obtaining gold from alluvial

* The following account of the discovery of " a hundredweight
of gold," from the *Sydney Morning Herald* of 18th July 1851,
is curious and worth preserving :—

" Bathurst is mad again !  The delirium of golden fever has
returned with increased intensity.  Men meet together, stare
stupidly at each other, talk incoherent nonsense, and wonder
what will happen next.  Everybody has a hundred times seen
a hundredweight of flour; a hundredweight of sugar or potatoes
is an everyday fact, but a hundredweight of gold is a phrase
scarcely known in the English language.  It is beyond the range
of our ordinary ideas, a sort of physical incomprehensibility, but
that it is a material existence our own eyes bore witness on
Monday last.

" Mr Suttor, a few days previously, threw out a few misty hints
about the possibility of a single individual digging *Four Thousand
Pounds worth of gold* in one day, but no one believed him serious.
It was thought that he was doing a little harmless puffing for
his own district and the Turon diggings.  On Sunday it began
to be whispered about town that Dr Kerr, Mr Suttor's brother-
in-law, had found *a hundredweight of gold.*  Some few believed

deposits, no complex machinery is employed, and little capital is needed.   In general hired labour is not trusted.

it, but the townspeople generally, and amongst the rest the writer of this article, treated the story as a piece of ridiculous exaggeration, and the bearer of it as a jester who gave the Bathurstonians unlimited credit for gullibility.   The following day, however, set the matter at rest.   About two o'clock in the afternoon, two greys, in tandem, driven by W. H. Suttor, Esq., M.C., made their appearance at the bottom of William Street. In a few seconds they were pulled up opposite the *Free Press* Office, and the first indication of the astounding fact which met the view was two massive pieces of the precious metal, glittering in virgin purity, as they leaped from the solid rock.   An intimation that the valuable prize was to reach the town on that day having been pretty generally circulated in the early part of the morning, the townspeople were on the *qui vive*, and in almost as little time as it has taken to write it, 150 people had collected around the gig conveying the time's wonder, eager to catch a glimpse of the monster lump said to form a portion of it.   The two pieces spoken of were freely handed about amongst the assembled throng for some twenty minutes.   Astonishment, wonder, incredulity, admiration, and the other kindred sentiments of the human heart, were depicted upon the features of all present in a most remarkable manner, and they were by no means diminished in intensity, when a square tin box in the body of the vehicle was pointed out as the repository of the remainder of the *hundredweight of gold*.   Having good-naturedly gratified the curiosity of the people, Mr Suttor invited us to accompany his party to the Union Bank of Australia to witness the interesting process of weighing.   We complied with alacrity, and the next

Every man works for himself; and a pick, a spade, and
a rinsing-box or cradle, are all the implements that are

moment the greys dashed off at a gallant pace, followed by a
hearty cheer from the multitude.

"In a few moments the tin box and its contents were placed on
the table of the Board Room of the Bank. In the presence of
the Manager, David Kennedy, W. H. Suttor, T. J. Hawkins,
Esqs., and the fortunate proprietor, Dr Kerr, the weighing com-
menced, Dr Machattie officiating and Mr Ferrand acting as clerk.
The first two pieces already alluded to weighed severally 6 lbs.
4 oz. 1 dwt., and 6 lbs. 13 dwts., besides which were sixteen
drafts of 5 lbs. 4 oz. each, making in all 102 lbs. 9 oz. 5 dwts.
From Dr Kerr we learned that he had retained upwards of 3 lbs.
as specimens, so that the total weight found would be 106 lbs.
(one hundred and six pounds)—all disembowelled from the earth
at one time. And now for the particulars of this extraordinary
gathering which has set the town and district in a whirl of ex-
citement.

"A few days ago, an educated aboriginal, formerly attached to
the Wellington Mission, and who has been in the service of W.
J. Kerr, Esq. of Wallawa, about seven years, returned home to
his employer with the intelligence that he had discovered a large
mass of gold amongst a heap of quartz upon the run whilst tending his sheep. Gold being the universal topic of conversation
the curiosity of this sable son of the forest was excited, and, provided with a tomahawk, he had amused himself by exploring the
country adjacent to his employer's land, and had thus made the
discovery. His attention was first called to the lucky spot by
observing a speck of some glittering yellow substance upon the
surface of a block of the quartz, upon which he applied his toma-

required.   Gold, in short, as now supplied to us from alluvial deposits, is perhaps more directly and immedi-

hawk, and broke off a portion.   At that moment the splendid prize stood revealed to his sight.   His first care was to start off home and disclose his discovery to his master, to whom he presented whatever gold might be procured from it.   As may be supposed, little time was lost by the worthy Doctor.   Quick as horseflesh would carry him he was on the ground, and in a very short period the three blocks of quartz, containing *the hundred-weight of gold*, were released from the bed where, charged with unknown wealth, they had rested perhaps for thousands of years, awaiting the hand of civilized man to disturb them.   The largest of the blocks was about a foot in diameter, and weighed 75 lbs. gross.   Out of this piece 60 lbs. of pure gold was taken.   Before separation it was beautifully encased in quartz.   The other two were something smaller.   The auriferous mass weighed as nearly as could be guessed from two to three cwt.   Not being able to move it conveniently, Dr Kerr broke the pieces into small fragments, and herein committed a very grand error.   As specimens the glittering blocks would have been invaluable.   Nothing yet known of would have borne comparison, or, if any, the comparison would have been in our favour.   From the description given by him, as seen in their original state, the world has seen nothing like them yet.

" The heaviest of the two large pieces presented an appearance not unlike a honeycomb or sponge, and consisted of particles of a crystalline form, as did nearly the whole of the gold.   The second larger piece was smoother, and the particles more condensed, and seemed as if it had been acted upon by water.   The remainder was broken into lumps of from two to three pounds

166 GOLD.

ately the product of human labour,—more exclusively
represents wages,—than any other commodity whatever.

and downwards, and were remarkably free from quartz or earthy
matter ; when heaped together on the table they presented a
splendid appearance, and shone with an effulgence calculated to
dazzle the brain of any man not armed with the coldness of
stoicism.

" The spot where this mass of treasure was found will be celebrated in the golden annals of these districts, and we shall therefore describe it as minutely as our means of information will
allow.  In the first place, the quartz blocks formed an isolated
heap, and were distant about 100 yards from a quartz vein which
stretches up the ridge from the Murroo Creek.  The locality is
the commencement of an undulating table-land, very fertile, and
is contiguous to a never-failing supply of water in the above
named creek.  It is distant about fifty-three miles from Bathurst,
eighteen from Mudgee, thirty from Wellington, and eighteen to
the nearest point of the Macquarie River, and is within about
eight miles of Dr Kerr's head station.  The neighbouring country
has been pretty well explored since the discovery, but with the
exception of dust, no further indications have been found.

" In return for his very valuable services, Dr Kerr has presented the black fellow and his brother with two flocks of sheep,
two saddle horses, and a quantity of rations, and supplied them
with a team of bullocks to plough some land in which they are
about to sow a crop of maize and potatoes.  One of the brothers,
mounted on a serviceable roadster, accompanied the party into
town, and appeared not a little proud of his share in the trans-
action.

" Our readers are now in possession of an accurate history of

"By far the richest deposit," says Lieutenant-Governor Latrobe, in his despatch to the Colonial Secretary of 10th October 1851, "is found in the small veins of blue clay, which lie almost above the so called 'pipe clay,' in which no trace of the ore has been discovered. The ore is to all appearance quite pure. It is found occasionally in rolled or waterworn irregular lumps of various sizes, from a quarter or half-an-ounce to one or two ounces in weight, sometimes incorporated with round pebbles of quartz, which appears to have formed its original matrix; at other times, without any admixture whatever, in irregular rounded or smooth pieces, and again in fused irregular masses of pure metal of great beauty, weighing in some instances seven or nine ounces. It is also found combined with quartz pebbles, or gravel of various sizes, evidently united to them while in a fused state, and on the surface of the de-

the whole affair. The particulars were kindly furnished by Mr Suttor and Dr Kerr, and may therefore be relied on as correct. Since the affair was blazoned to the world, several gentlemen of our acquaintance have shown undoubted symptoms of temporary insanity, and the nerves of the community at large have sustained a severe shock. Should the effect be at all proportionate in Sydney to its population, the inmates of Bedlam Point may be fairly reckoned an integral portion of the community."

tached masses of iron sandstone, but in the greatest
abundance in the clays, from which it is washed in the
form of rounded or flattened grains, like sifted gravel
and sand of varied sizes.  These will, however, be frequently seen to be interspersed with larger pieces, either
pure or combined with quartz, as before described.  I
have met with no instances in this locality of the form
commonly called ' scale gold.'  The seams of the auriferous blue clay, the general position of which I have
described, are found to be most irregular in their deposit, and seldom more than four or five inches in
thickness.  They appear, disappear, and break off and
thin out continually.  The closest proximity to a rich
vein in an adjacent working can afford no certain as-
surance that the labour of the adventurer will be sim-
ilarly rewarded.  I may give you some idea of the
value of this partial deposit, however, when hit upon,
by stating that I witnessed, during my visit, the washing of two tin dishes of this clay, of about twenty inches
in diameter, the yield of which was no less than eight
pounds weight of pure gold, and I have seen two or at
most three cubic inches of the same yield four ounces.''*

* Farther Papers relative to the recent Discovery of Gold in
Australia, presented to Parliament, 14th June 1852, p. 44.

The cost of producing gold, therefore, depends mainly on the productiveness of the manual labour directly employed in digging and washing.  The work is hard no doubt, and the returns more precarious and fluctuating than in other employments.  But when allowance is made for these drawbacks, it is astonishing how soon the earnings of workmen in all departments of industry equalize themselves.  Labourers in other employments soon come to know the average remuneration which miners, one month with another, or one year with another, can earn.*  If their own employment is less

* The following approximate estimate of the average earnings of the miners is given in an able article on "The Gold Discoveries," in the Quarterly Review for September last : "Taking the actual amount shipped from Melbourne to the end of March last, and allowing for the quantity supposed to be at the diggings and waiting shipment, it would appear that about 700,000 ounces had been raised in Victoria.   At £3 per ounce this would be worth £2,100,000.   The licenses issued up to the same date were 49,386. Dividing the gold by this number we get £42, 10s. as the average monthly earnings of each licensed digger ; but as a great number of persons evaded payment of the license fee, the real earnings of the diggers must have been considerably less.   In New South Wales the government regulations were more strictly enforced. The amount raised there to the end of March may be taken at 320,000 ounces, and the value at £960,000.   The licenses issued

severe, more steady, and attended with fewer risks and fluctuations, they will consent to take less wages than they could earn as miners, but only so much less as in their estimatiom is equal to the additional toil, hardship, and inconvenience which they escape by continuing at their former employments. Thus, according to late accounts, able-bodied labourers in California are receiving 100 dollars (or about £20) a-month with ample rations, while a quarter of wheat and four ounces of gold ore, estimated by the labour which they cost, are of equal value.*  In New South Wales and Victoria, where the wages of shepherds and servants in husbandry were formerly about £25 a-year with rations, they are now doubled or tripled.

I shall not stop to notice the numerous communications which have been addressed to the metropolitan, provincial, and colonial newspapers by private adventurers during the last twelve months, and which are

were 30,781, and by the same rule these figures give £31, 3s. as the monthly average, which is probably very near the truth, the most intelligent of the commissioners commonly speaking of £1 per day as the digger's earnings."—*Quarterly Review for September* 1852, p. 521.

* Quarterly Review for March 1852, p. 497.

now lying before me in hundreds.*  I shall confine
myself chiefly to official sources of information, and

* The following extracts are from the private letter of an Indian
officer upon sick-leave, which appeared lately in the *Times:*—

"*Melbourne, June* 18.

.    .    .    .    .    .    .    .    .    .    .    .

"Gold is being found in greater quantities than ever. . As the
winter advances, food and necessaries will increase in price.
They are already very high, the roads are cut up, and the creeks
and rivers swollen.  It is supposed there are upwards of 40,000
people at the different diggings.  The price of everything is exorbitant.  Any man with some money might double it with the
greatest ease and safety every month ; but as to men on incomes
of £150 to £200 a-year, the commonest workmen are in a better
position.  A common carter makes £12 a-week; his expenses
perhaps are £4.  A cab or rather carriage driver, makes £30 to
£40 a-week, or above £1400 a-year.  Masons and carpenters receive £1 a-day, but they won't work even for this.  There is
nothing of any kind going on.  All houses or public buildings
that were in progress are now at a stand-still.  No one can get
servants.  The Chief-Justice told me that his had left him months
ago.  His son opened the door to us, and I believe his wife (as
many other ladies have had to do) washes her own clothes.  The
Governor has no servants ; every man is so independent that they
will not hire themselves to do anything unless they get what they
ask.  Going into a shop, if you ask them to abate in their exorbitant price, they quietly tell you to walk out, that they don't
want to sell anything to you.  A load of water is 18s.; a load of
wood £4; boots are £4; a pair of shoes £2; jack-boots, which
are much used at the diggings, £7.  Pistols fetch any amount.

shall quote to you the Despatches embodied in the *Papers relating to the recent Discovery of Gold in Aus-*

An invoice, valued at £60, arrived a short time since ; in a week's time they were all sold, having realized nearly £700. The way they generally go to the diggings is this :—They form themselves into parties of three or four, buy a cart and two or three horses, load it with everything that is necessary for their living and working for two or three months, according to their own pleasure. Some men clear £300 or £400 a-month, some not so much ; some have done more. There is one just returned, and now in the hotel, who was away six weeks and cleared £3600 ; but the real way to make money is buying gold, if you have any capital. At the diggings it sells for £2, 15s. and £2, 17s. an ounce ; in Melbourne, for £3, 5s. per ounce. The gold is sent down by escort, and can be realized, and the sovereigns sent by the return escort ; therefore 8s. to 10s. may be made on every ounce twice-a month. This is the way the banks and all the houses are making immense sums. The escort arrives every week. They brought more gold last time than they ever have before, above 55,000 ounces. There is also a private escort which brings down large quantities ; private hands also bring a good deal.     .     .     .     .     .

" Draught horses are all bought up here immediately they are heard of. We have a cart, and are trying to get two cart-horses to start with. We hoped to have got away yesterday, but could not procure horses. We have got all things ready, a small tent, cooking things, a cradle, pickaxes, shovels, &c., and a cart. All the things are moderate except the latter, and that is £40. They ask £60 a-piece for a moderately good cart horse ; six months ago they went for £10 and £15! We were offered a pair yesterday for £185, but that we could not give. A cart is absolutely

*tralia,* which were presented to both Houses of Parliament, by command of her Majesty, in June last.   The Lieutenant-Governor of Victoria, in his despatch of 3d December 1851,* represents the progress and results of the successful search for gold in that part of Australia as tending "completely to disorganize the whole structure of society.  The discovery of gold in a pure state, it is added, not only under the surface, but in many instances upon the very surface, requiring but little or no labour to collect; and the enormous gains made in many instances after a few days' or even hours' labour, clear

necessary to cart the soil to the water, besides taking our things up.   If we can get a horse to-morrow we shall be off on Monday to the diggings—to the Bendigo—and try our luck for a month or so. . . . . .

"The rent of houses here is immense; for one of four or five rooms unfurnished, you pay £350 and £400.   All the poor Government officials—from the Governor downwards—are being ruined, and unless their salaries are raised out of the increased revenue derived from the gold-fields, many of them will be in a most painful position.   The average salaries are from £300 to £400 per year, not so much as some of the smallest houses rent for.   Lodgings cannot be had under £5 per week.   You may imagine what other expenses are from this."—*For still later Accounts, see Note at the end of the Volume.*

* Farther Papers relative to the recent Discovery of Gold in Australia, presented to Parliament, 14th June 1852, p. 51.

proof of which is seen in the large amounts brought
down by the government escort, and by private individuals, could have no other effect, and at this moment
it really becomes a question how the more sober operations of society, and even the functions of government,
may be carried on."

In his next despatch, of date 19th December 1851,
Mr Latrobe says,* "The gold raised upon the Mount
Alexander gold-fields is now calculated by hundred-
weights, and arrives in the cities by the government
escort, or private conveyance, at the rate of probably
two tons per week—so it has been at least for the last
two weeks.  Some 20,000 individuals are calculated to
be congregated at the principal fields in that quarter,
now four in number, and scattered over the adjacent
country on a space of twenty miles square.  A large
proportion of the numbers actually working are making
large profits, and on all hands undoubted proofs of the
easy acquisition of great wealth by the labouring classes
abound.  A pound weight of gold a-day is small remuneration for a party, and many secure five or six,
and there are instances of as much as fifty being the
result of but a few hours' labour.  Large quantities have

* Farther Papers, &c., p. 62.

likewise been scraped from the very surface. Even where the ore lies beneath it, having been deposited under the alluvion, immediately above and in the fissures of the slate rock, the labour of reaching it is trifling compared with that at Ballarat."

The consequence of these unprecedented discoveries of alluvial gold has been a great and sudden rise in the wages of labour, in the prices of provisions and colonial products generally, and in the salaries of government and other officials. Gold, obtained as above described, being the direct product of labour, without the intervention of capital (at least of any considerable amount of capital), has had the effect which *a priori* we should have expected, of instantly raising wages,* and,

---

* The comparative rates of wages in 1850 and 1851 are thus stated in one of the papers referred to in Mr Latrobe's despatch of 12th January 1852 :—The wages of shearers rose from 12s. in 1850 to 20s. in 1851; of reapers, from 10s. to 20s. and 25s. per acre ; of common labourers, from 5s. to 15s. and 20s. per day ; of coopers, from 5s. to 10s. ; of shipwrights, from 6s. to 10s. ; woolpressers, from 3s. 6d. to 7s. and 8s. per day ; sailors, from £4 to £9 a-month—(from £50 to £100 being offered for the run to England) ; stokers, from £12 to £20 a-month ; men cooks, from 20s. and 25s. to £2 and £3 a-week ; waiters at hotels, from 20s. to 40s. and 50s. a-week ; ostlers and stable-men, from 21s. to 50s. a-week ; men-servants in town, from £25 and £30 to £50 and £70 per annum, and none to be had even at these exorbitant wages ;

through wages, the prices of all commodities in the colony.

men-servants in the country, from £20 and £25 to £35 and £40; salesmen, shopmen, &c., from 25s. and 35s. to 40s. and 70s. a-week; porters, from 12s. and 15s. to 25s. and 35s. a-week; female servants, 25 per cent.; clerks in banks and mercantile houses, 20 to 50 per cent.; artisans, &c., 80 to 120 per cent.

From December 1850 to December 1851, the prices of provisions, &c. had risen as follows:—Bread, 4 lb. loaf, from 5d. to 1s. 4d. and 1s. 8d.; butter, from 1s. 2d. to 2s. and 2s. 6d.; cheese, from 8d. and 1s. 4d. to 2s. and 3s.; fresh meat doubled; salt meat, from 1½d. to 2½d.; ham, from 8d. and 1s. to 1s. 6d. and 2s. 6d.; bacon, from 6d. and 8d. to 2s. per lb.; fowls and ducks, from 3s. and 3s. 6d. to 5s. and 6s. a couple; potatoes, from 8s. to 12s. and 15s. a cwt.; tobacco, from 2s. 6d. and 4s. to 7s. and 8s. a lb.; groceries generally 25 per cent.; vegetables, from 50 to 100 per cent.; spirits, wine, beer, &c., from 30 to 50 per cent.; confectionary, 50 per cent.; fruit, 100 per cent.

The following are the per-centage rates of increase on the prices of some of the supplies furnished under contracts for the government service of Victoria:—Candles, 60 per cent.; fresh beef, 33⅓ per cent.; salt pork, 25 per cent.; bread, 50 per cent.; tea, about 21 per cent.; sugar, 10 per cent.; soap, 20 per cent.; milk, 75 per cent.; new horse-shoes, 150 per cent.; cost of removing old ones, 350 per cent.; printing, 100 per cent.; saddlery, 75 per cent.; for boots and shoes no tenders could be obtained; "*old* furniture," it is added, "sells at about 75 per cent. advance upon the former price of *new;* scarcely any mechanic will work, those few who do, receive an advance on former wages of 200 per cent. to carpenters, and 350 per cent. to blacksmiths.—*Farther Papers*, &c., pp. 80, 81.

Australia being the first example in history of the discovery of abundant gold-fields in the midst of a civilized and intelligent community, already possessed of capital, and having its industry organized and protected by a stable government and free institutions, we are in the most favourable position to mark the action of great accessions of metallic wealth upon the money value of labour and commodities.   The phenomena, in as far as they have yet developed themselves, have occurred exactly in the order that might have been expected.   First of all we have had a rise in the money price of colonial labour; next in the price of provisions, and the other direct products of that labour;* and, lastly, and after a greater interval, we may expect to witness an elevation of the money value of commodities imported into the colony, with a corresponding rise of prices in England

---

* The following prices of labour and of provisions are given in *Westgarth & Company's Price-Current*, dated *Melbourne, 1st June* 1852 :—" Day-labourers, 8s. to 10s. per day; carpenters, 20s. a-day; masons and other artisans, 12s. to 15s. a-day; shepherds, with rations, &c., £40 to £50 per annum; men servants, £60 per annum; female servants, £35 to £40 per annum; wheat, 7s. per bushel; oats, 7s. per bushel; barley, 6s. per bushel; bacon, 1s. 8d.; cheese, 1s.; butter, 1s. 6d. to 1s. 9d. per lb.; bread, 4 lb. loaf, 1s. 4d.; beef and mutton, 3d. per lb."

and the other countries whence these imported commodities are derived. A longer time will be required
for the development of this last effect, but it is not the
less certain to occur.

That a rise or fall of money wages, proceeding from
an alteration of the conditions under which the metal
which forms the standard of money is produced, will be
followed by a corresponding elevation or depression of
the money prices of all the products of labour, is allowed
by Mr Ricardo, whose doctrine is, that a rise or fall of
wages has generally no effect whatever upon the price
of commodities. "Money being a variable commodity,"
he says, "the rise of money wages will be frequently
occasioned by a fall in the value of money. A rise of
wages *from this cause*, will, indeed, be invariably accompanied by a rise in the price of commodities; but
in such cases it will be found that labour and all commodities have not varied in regard to each other, and
that the variation has been confined to money."* And,
again, "a rise in wages, from an alteration in the value
of money, produces a general effect on price."†

In England, and in countries where the precious

* Ricardo's Political Works (M'Culloch's Edition), p. 31.
† Ib.

metals are imported commodities, we should expect the order of the phenomena consequent on the gold discoveries to be the reverse of what we see taking place in Australia and California. In Europe there will probably be first of all a rise in the price of provisions and of commodities generally, followed, at but a short interval, by a corresponding rise in the money price of labour.

You must not misunderstand me so far as to suppose, that I intend to advocate any such heterodox doctrine as that the value of gold is determined by laws different from those which regulate the permanent value of silver. On the contrary, nothing can be clearer than that the self-same law determines, and must determine, the value of both. The originating cause in both cases is the same, and the ultimate effect is the same. But as regards the *time* required to produce the effects, a distinction I think must be made; and you are not rashly to conclude, that because silver,—a commodity which, like iron, cannot be produced without the agency of extensive capital, and the cost of producing which after the discovery of the more abundant mines of America was regulated mainly by the comparative abundance of mercury, and the progressive advancement of science and the arts,—did not materially affect general prices in Europe for more than half a century—the same, or any thing like the same, period must elapse before gold—a commodity produced under very different conditions, produced chiefly by the agency of direct labour, without the intervention of much capital, and generally in a state of almost virgin purity—will create a great, permanent, and universal elevation of prices in all the markets of the world.

## LETTER XIX.

*Supplies of gold in the early part of the present century—supplies since the discovery of the Russian, Californian, and Australian deposits—Coinage of gold, and its consumption in the arts—Future prospects.*

BEFORE adverting to the circumstances which determine the permanent value of the precious metals in countries which do not produce them, but into which they are imported by the operations of commerce, let us take a rapid glance at the comparative amount of the importations of gold at the commencement of the present century, and before and after the discovery of the Russian, Californian, and Australian gold-fields.

The whole amount of the precious metals in the world has been estimated by some at two thousand millions sterling, while others have supposed that Europe and America alone possess a stock of more than seventeen hundred millions.* The amount of specie in circulation throughout the world has been variously computed at from £340,000,000 to £400,000,000, of which three-eighths are supposed to consist of gold, and the remaining five-eighths of silver. These estimates are founded upon no *data* that can be relied upon, and they must be regarded as mere conjectures. Political arithmetic is here completely at fault. We may guess more or less plausibly, but that is all. The nature of the thing does not admit of satisfactory evidence; and no conclusion can be safely deduced from premises, which, notwithstanding their air of numerical precision, are really nothing better than random assumptions and surmises.

Baron Humboldt estimates the average annual produce of gold and silver in America, Europe, and Northern Asia, at the commencement of the present century, at somewhat over ten millions sterling, of which sum £2,612,200 are supposed to have consisted of gold. This annual supply was continued, and even increased,

---

* A writer in the Morning Chronicle estimates the quantity of gold in Europe and America in the beginning of 1848 at about 560 millions sterling, and of silver 1170 millions—together 1730 millions sterling.

down to 1810, when the War of Independence broke out.  The struggle between Spain and her colonies, and the violence and insecurity and destruction of capital which were its attendants, led to the abandonment of many of the mines, and a great falling off in the annual supply.  From 1810 to 1830, Mr Jacob computes the average produce of the American mines at less than one half of the former amount, or £4,036,838.  After this, an improvement took place, and Mr M'Culloch estimates* the annual produce of the American mines in 1843 at £5,600,000.  In 1846 it reached £6,563,179.

More than thirty years ago supplies of gold began to be received from Russia, and these supplies have since progressively increased.  In 1837 the produce was only £900,673 ; in 1847 it was £3,700,000.†   In 1850, £4,175,800.‡  In 1851, the yield has been computed at only 64,932 lbs. troy ; § but as a much less quantity is exported than is actually raised, there seems no reason to conclude that the average is materially declining.

In September 1847, golden treasures, till then un-

* Dictionary of Commerce—*v.* Precious Metals.

† Supplement to M'Culloch's Commercial Dictionary—Art. Gold.

‡ Mr Birkmyre's Tables—Times, 21st May 1852.

§ History and Statistics of Gold, by R. Hunt, Esq., p. 198.

equalled in the history of the world, were discovered in California. In the succeeding year, the estimated exports of gold were from £800,000 to £1,000,000; next year, they increased to £4,000,000: in 1850, to £12,000,000,—a sum not far from equal to the estimated annual produce of all the gold and silver mines in the world before the Californian discoveries; while last year the exports exceeded £17,000,000, and during the present year there seems no reason to doubt that they will reach the astonishing sum of Twenty Millions sterling!*

In February 1851, rich gold-fields were discovered in the territory of New South Wales, and in August following still richer and apparently inexhaustible deposits were found in the colony of Victoria. These have since been worked by thousands of labourers; and, according to a well-informed writer in the Times,† the produce of gold from Australia alone during the present year is not likely to fall short of £6,000,000; while other writers,

* See Mr Birkmyre's Tables in *Times*, May 21, 1852. The official deposits of gold from California, at the various United States Mints, are thus stated in Hussey & Co's Circular of 30th June 1852:—

| | | | | |
|---|---|---|---|---|
| 1848, | . | . | . | 44,177 dollars. |
| 1849, | . | . | . 6,147,509 | „ |
| 1850, | . | . | . 36,074,062 | „ |
| 1851, | . | . | . 55,938,232 | „ |

† Times, 21st May 1851—Tables by Mr Birkmyre.

proceeding upon more recent information, estimate the probable yield at a much higher sum.*

* See Quarterly Review for September 1852.

As these sheets are passing through the press, the following statement has appeared in the *Times:*—"For about two years the rule of Australian intelligence has been that the latest accounts not only confirmed those before, but cast them into the shade. How long this ratio of progression is to go on, we do not venture to guess, nor is it at all necessary, for we have only to suppose the yield of gold, actual, ascertained, and regular, at the last date, to continue for some years without further increase, and there is enough to justify the wildest speculations as to commercial and social results. At the last date, the weekly produce of one gold district, seventy miles from Melbourne, was near 100,000 ounces, equivalent to £20,000,000 a-year; and, at a moderate estimate, the whole yearly produce of Australia would not be less than £40,000,000. As a natural consequence, Australian society had revolved itself into one great association of diggers. In Victoria, or Port-Phillip as it used to be called, the men, with a few strong-minded women, to the number of about 60,000, were at work on the various operations immediately necessary for getting at the gold, while many thousands were engaged in subsidiary employments. Ordinary occupations were neglected. The cattle were driven to the diggings from the distance of hundreds of miles, not as before to be shorn for their wool, or killed for their tallow, the rest being thrown away; but to be killed for their meat, the skins and wool being now the indisposable refuse, and being accordingly burnt on the spot. Wages for all kinds of labour had risen, to keep pace with the profits of gold hunting; and carriage from Melbourne to the diggings was £100 a-ton, or

Look, then, at the case as it stands.   In 1846, two
years before the Californian mines were discovered, the

even higher.   Of course very great inducements were required
to prevent sailors from deserting, and to get ships out of port.
The population of Melbourne had already increased to such an
extent, that thousands were living in tents in the surrounding
fields, and the cry was 'Still they come.'   How far that expec-
tation was likely to be further fulfilled, we in this country have
some means of judging.   It is estimated that in the course of this
year, 100,000 persons will have left the British Isles for the different Australian colonies, nearly all of these, first or last, destined
to reach, if not the diggings, at least the neighbouring dependent
cities.   The greater part of these 100,000 are already on their
way in mid-sea, and in the southern hemisphere.   The rest are
certain to follow.   The above are not probabilities, but facts."

The most recent accounts are thus noticed in the City Article
of the *Times* of 23d November 1852 :—" The advices from Port-
Phillip (Victoria) by the Eagle, are to the 2d September, nearly
two months later than those previously received ; but owing to
the absence of any summary of the amounts of gold brought
into Melbourne each week, it is impossible to obtain from them
any precise estimate of the general yield.   They indicate, however, that there had been no falling off, and that the animation
and confidence of all parties in the colony was daily increasing.
The only week in which the totals brought by escort are given,
is that ending the 7th August, when they amounted to 105,000
ounces.   Owing to the irregularities of the government escort, large
quantities were brought by private hand.   The total exported to
England, from the date of the first discoveries up to the 31st of
July, was 1,265,640 ounces, or about £5,000,000, from Victoria,

produce of all the gold and silver mines of the world
(exclusive of China and Japan) was . £12,362,677

In 1850, two years after that discovery, it was . . . . . 27,442,788
_____

Increase over 1846, . £15,080,111*
_____

while from New South Wales, up to the 14th August, it was
£2,007,012, at the colonial price of 65s. per ounce, or about
£2,500,000 actual value. Of this latter sum, however, a considerable portion was from Victoria, so that there was no comparison
between the production of the respective colonies. A further
total of not less than £1,000,000 had been forwarded also from
Victoria to Adelaide, South Australia. The people from Adelaide
were universally the most successful, owing to their previous
familiarity with mining pursuits, and an instance is mentioned
of one party having realized £6000 in a single morning. New
deposits were constantly announced, a place called Koorong,
about thirty miles from Bendigo, and another called Anderson's
Creek, near Melbourne, being among the most prolific spots.
Some fresh fields in the neighbourhood of Ballarat are also mentioned as realizing the highest anticipations. The price of gold had
risen to 67s. 6d. in consequence of the arrival of about £200,000
in coin (chiefly by the Peninsular and Oriental Company's steamer
Chusan, which left England on the 15th May), and the expec-
tation of further supplies. The prosperity of the miners, and
the probability of the ultimate establishment of a mint, caused
also an indisposition to make hasty sales. The rapidly accumu-

* Times, 21st May 1852—Mr Birkmyre's Tables.

In 1852, taking the most moderate estimates which have been formed, it is not unlikely to reach £43,000,000,

lating wealth of all classes was manifested in a growing disposition to undertake important and costly enterprises.  A bill had been introduced in the Victoria Legislature for a railway to run from Melbourne to Mount Alexander, which it was anticipated would cost near £1,000,000.  It was also projected to connect Melbourne with the port at Hobson's Bay by a short line, and to construct a pier, where the largest vessels could unload, the proposed capital being £100,000.  A new bank to be called the Bank of Victoria, with a capital of £1,000,000, had at the same time been projected.  There was a scheme, moreover, before the New South Wales legislature, for a railway from Sydney to Melbourne, a distance of 600 miles.  The last advices received at Port-Phillip from England were to the 2d June, but the mail-steamer Australian was just entering when the Eagle left with Plymouth dates to the 5th of that month.  From Sydney the latest accounts by the present arrival are to the 23d August.  A motion for establishing a small mint was to be brought forward on the following day, and was expected to pass immediately, so that the materials might be obtained from England forthwith.  Port Jackson had been declared a free port, the Royal assent to the requisite act having been received.  According to intelligence from Honolulu, a considerable emigration might be expected from the Sandwich Islands.  From South Australia news had been received the day before the sailing of the Eagle, that the long-desired discovery of gold had taken place in that colony, a very extensive field having been pointed out about fifteen miles from Adelaide to the south-east.  Most of the experiments made on the surface had thus far been satisfactory.  Large remittances from Mount Alex-

being an increase over 1846 of £30,637,323, and over 1850 of £15,557,212 sterling.

The produce of California alone, from the commencement of mining operations in 1848 to 30th June 1852, is computed by parties on the spot to amount to 174,780,877 dollars, or, taking the dollar at 4s., to £34,956,175 sterling.*

These unparalleled supplies have added more than thirty millions sterling to the stock of bullion which was held by the banks of England, France, and New York, in 1848.

" The average yearly coinage of gold during the first thirty years of this century," according to Mr Birkmyre,

ander continued to be received at the Assay-office at Adelaide, and it was in contemplation to coin tokens of 20s. each, the government assayer having been instructed to engage the requisite staff and machinery for that purpose. The Burra Burra Mine Shares were steadily supported, and the price appears to have ranged between 130 and 135.

"The Pelham has arrived to-day from Sydney, whence she sailed the 17th of July with 27,761 ounces of gold, valued at £111,000. The Oceanie, which sailed about the same date, has also been announced, but the amount she has brought cannot be correctly ascertained."

* Hussey, Bond, and Hale's Circular, San Francisco, 30th July 1852.

" was in Great Britain £1,700,000; France, £1,300,000;
in the United States, £55,000 ; total, £3,055,000." The
following is a statement of the recent gold coinage in
the same countries, beginning with the year in which
the gold discovery was made in California :—

|  | Great Britain. | France. | United States. | Total. |
|---|---|---|---|---|
| 1848, . . | £2,451,999 | £1,234,472 | £786,565 | £4,473,036 |
| 1849, . . | 2,177,000 | 1,084,382 | 1,875,158 | 5,136,540 |
| 1850, . . | 1,491,000 | 3,407,691 | 6,662,854 | 11,561,545 |
| 1851, . . | (10 months) | 10,077,252 | 12,919,695 | |

From November 1850 to June 1851, the Bank of
England issued 9,500,000 sovereigns, and since November 1851, 3,500,000 sovereigns and half-sovereigns.*
The annual consumption of the precious metals has
been variously estimated, and has given rise to much
difference of opinion.    I am disposed to follow rather
the computation of Mr M'Culloch than that of Mr Jacob.
Mr M'Culloch, in 1843, estimated the annual value of
the precious metals used in the arts at £6,050,000, but
of this amount he assumed that one-fifth, or 20 per cent.,
was obtained from the fusion of old plate, &c.  The actual
consumption of the metals, therefore, for purposes of
ornament and luxury, he makes £4,840,000, while he

* History and Statistics of Gold, by R. Hunt, Esq., p. 203, 204.

adds one per cent. of the amount used as coin for tear
and wear, and loss by fire and shipwreck.  Assuming
the amount of specie in circulation in the world to be
£340,000,000, we must therefore deduct one per cent.,
or  .   .   .   .   .   .   .   £3,400,000
Add annual consumption as above, for
   other purposes than coin,   .   .   4,840,000

We have thus a total consumption of  .  £8,240,000
against an annual produce of   .   .  43,000,000

Leaving an annual accumulation for the
   purposes of money of   .   .   .  £34,760,000

—a sum nearly three times greater than the gross annual
produce prior to the recent discoveries!

That these extraordinary supplies of a metal which
forms the sole standard of our money, the universal
medium of exchange, and the common measure of commerce, in relation to which all pecuniary contracts are
adjusted, and the value of all commodities is estimated,
—a metal, too (unlike silver), produced by the simplest
means, in a state ready for the market the day after it
is dug from the earth or washed from the sands, and at
almost no other cost than the manual labour employed

in gathering it,—that these supplies if continued will produce a rise of prices in England and in all countries using a gold standard to an extent of which recent times furnish no example,—it seems impossible for any one accustomed to think upon such subjects to entertain a reasonable doubt.*

* That these supplies will be continued for very many years to come, there seems equally little reason to doubt. Labourers are now emigrating to the gold regions in thousands and tens of thousands, while the fields opened to their industry would seem to be unbounded. Mr Lyman, in his " Notes on the Californian Gold Regions," tells us, " That the gold region is a longitudinal strip or tract from ten to forty miles in width, and extending in length a distance of many hundred miles ; active operations being already (1849) carried on through an extent of 400 or 500 miles at least." Equally extensive, or still more so, are the Australian gold-fields. " Judging," says Mr Latrobe, " from the general pre-valence of the geological formation in which the gold has hitherto been found so abundantly over the whole length and breadth of the colony, *I can contemplate no limit to the discoveries, or the re-sults of the opening of these fields.*"—*Despatch* of 19th December 1851. Mr Hardy, the chief gold commissioner, in his official report, says, " In the whole course of the Turon River the pro-duction of gold appears to be as regular as wheat in a sown field. In short, from the top of the bank, across the whole bed of the river (from 50 to 100 yards wide), and for the whole nine miles that I have examined it, the result is as absolutely to be depended on as weekly wages, and 5000 workers would be nothing in that

space. . . . . I do not think that there is a spot on any part of the Turon on which an industrious and careful man may not earn 10s. per day, while the great majority of such men may earn from 15s. to £1 each per day.  I know a large number of men who earn £2 each per day; and there is equally profitable digging ground on this river, now unoccupied, for several thousands.  In fact I can at present see no limit to the number of persons that may be employed; for I have ascertained by personal observation that the numerous creeks, many of them ten or fifteen miles long, that fall into the Turon, produce gold at the rate of about 10s. to each man per day.  Three men in that locality have in this and the three preceding days obtained 10 lbs. weight of gold (about £400) in pieces not exceeding 1 oz. in weight.  The average earnings of the 200 men who took out licenses on these creeks are not less than £1 a-day each."  These accounts are confirmed by Mr Stuchbury, the colonial geologist, who adds, " that there is scarcely a gully or creek which, upon careful examination, does not produce gold."—See a pamphlet entitled *The Colonies of Australia, their Formation, Progress, and Present State,* by John Fairfax, Esq., joint-proprietor and joint-editor of the Sydney Morning Herald, p. 43.

The following notice of the astounding quantities of gold which are now being imported from Australia appears in the *Times* of 24th November 1852:—" Yesterday three vessels arrived in the river Thames from Australia with the extraordinary quantity of upwards of seven tons of gold on board.  One of the ships, the Eagle, was freighted with the largest amount of the precious metal ever known to arrive in one vessel, viz. 150,000 ounces (upwards of six tons), and of the value of more than £600,000. The Eagle also made the most rapid passage on record, having done the voyage from Melbourne to the Downs in seventy-six days. The other ships are the Sapphire, from Sydney, with 14,668 ounces on board, and the Pelham, from Sydney, with 27,762 ounces. The Maitland also arrived a day or two since from Sydney, with 14,326 ounces. Great, however, as has been the wealth brought over by the Eagle, the ship Dido is expected in a few days, which will far surpass it, having on board 280,000 ounces, or about ten tons and a half of the precious metal. The Neptune, with 17,000 ounces; the Andromache, 42,051 ounces; and other ships, with as valuable freights, are nearly due."

# LETTER XX.

*Produce of silver—value of that metal in relation*
*to gold.*

THAT the produce of silver is increasing, and the cost
of producing it diminishing, concurrently with the unparalleled influx of the more valuable metal, is a fact
of great significance.   By this means the action of the
gold discoveries on the price of silver will be retarded,
but their action on the prices of other commodities in
countries where gold is the standard will not be thereby
diminished.

Before the discovery of America the value of silver
in relation to gold was as 11·158 to 1.   In what relation
the supply of the one metal then stood to that of the
other we have now no means of ascertaining.   Down
to 1525 the principal importations into Europe were of
gold.   From that period till the discovery of the mines
of Brazil in the beginning of the eighteenth century the

silver imported exceeded the gold in the ratio of 60 to 1. After that the proportion was reduced to 22 to 1. But from 1750 to 1800 it again rose to 40 to 1.*

From the reign of Charles the Second to that of George the First, the value of gold in relation to silver was not fixed by authority. Silver was then the sole standard of our money, and the value of a guinea fluctuated like that of any other commodity. Prior to the reformation of the silver coin in William the Third's reign, it varied from 20s. to 30s. In 1717 the relation of gold to silver was fixed by authority in the proportion of 15·209 to 1, in other words, 21s. were equivalent to a guinea. After this, we had a double standard, and both metals were legal tender, gold by tale, and silver also by tale to the amount of £25, and by weight, at the mint price, for any greater sum. In this adjustment, gold, as compared with silver, was overvalued; and it became consequently the interest of all debtors to pay in gold rather than in silver. Silver coins of full weight were by this means driven out of the market or melted, and gold came practically to be the standard by which all values were measured and all

* Humboldt's Political Essay on New Spain (Black's Translation), vol. iii. p. 435.

covenants adjusted.   In 1816, gold, in all payments
above 40s., was made the only legal tender, and silver
a subsidiary currency, bearing the same relation to gold
that copper does to silver.   A pound troy of silver
bullion has since been coined into 66s. instead of 62s.,
and its coinage charged with a seignorage of $6\frac{14}{31}$ per
cent.—in other words, the person who carries a pound
of silver to the mint gets back only 62s. of the 66s.
into which it is coined, and government retains the
power to coin more or less silver as may seem expedient.
Thus the sovereign containing 123·274 grains troy of
gold 22 carats fine, or 113·001 grains of pure gold, and
a shilling containing 87·2727 grains of standard silver,
or 80·727 grains of pure silver, the relation of the one
metal to the other at the mint is 14·28784 to 1, or
nearly $14\frac{2}{7}$ to 1.   The silver coin has now, therefore,
ceased to be a standard of value, and, like copper, serves
merely to facilitate smaller exchanges.   Gold at present
is our sole standard, minted at the rate of £3, 17s. $10\frac{1}{2}$d.,
and purchased by the Bank of England at £3, 17s. 9d.
an ounce, of 22 carats or $\frac{11}{12}$ths fine.

At the beginning of the present century, the produce
of silver in America was to that of gold as 46 to 1,
while in Europe the proportion was as 40 to 1.

In 1846, when the importations of gold from Russia had reached nearly 3½ millions, but before the discovery of the Californian deposits, the produce of the two metals is estimated at 727 tons of silver and 42 tons of gold; the relative supply of the one metal to that of the other being therefore as 17 to 1. But in 1850 the produce of silver was 978 tons and of gold 134 tons, and the proportion was consequently reduced to 7 to 1; while in 1851 the produce of silver is estimated at 1002 tons, of gold 180 tons, and the proportion still farther reduced to 5 to 1.*

As yet, there has been little or no change in the relative value of the two metals, silver being still sold in the market at 5s. or 5s. 1d. an ounce, and the silver coin continuing to circulate along with the gold coin, although large exportations of the former are beginning to take place.†

---

* See Statement by Mr Birkmyre, in Times, 21st May 1852.

† As long as our silver coins continue to circulate along with the gold coins, there seems no reason to expect that any material alteration of the *price* of silver will take place. The fact that twenty shillings can at any time be obtained for a sovereign, will of itself keep the value of silver from rising beyond a specified limit in relation to gold. But how long the silver coin will continue to circulate along with the gold coin is a different question.

While the annual supply of gold has been increasing, that of silvèr has not been stationary, although the proportional increase of the latter has been very much less

That a great displacement of silver has already taken place, in England as elsewhere, there seems no room to doubt.  The amount of silver held by the Bank of England in September 1846 was £2,710,077, which, however, included the sycee silver from China.  By the return for the week ending 23d October last, the stock of silver was reduced to £19,154.  The Times of 28th October stated authoritatively that, since the beginning of July last, "more than three million pieces of silver coin, to the value of upwards of £160,000, had been issued from the mint to the public through the Bank, and that the most energetic measures were being adopted at the mint to increase the supply."  Yet silver continues as scarce as ever.  If gold is to be continued as the sole measure of value, and should its value continue to fall in relation to silver, it seems quite obvious that we cannot retain our silver unless the mint proportions of the two metals be greatly altered.  The standard of silver must be lowered as has been done in America—a measure which would entail injustice on no one, seeing that since 1816 silver has been merely a subsidiary currency—legal tender to the extent of only 40s., and that all pecuniary contracts have been adjusted with reference to gold alone.  Our silver coins at present are by law mere counters or tokens to facilitate minor exchanges, and might like the copper coins be debased without detriment to commerce.  Nor is there any necessity why silver should be legal tender for more than twenty shillings.  If silver according to the present proportions be a better remittance than gold to countries which

than that of the former. Not only so, but we begin once more to have signs of a permanent diminution of the cost of producing silver. For three centuries the chief supplies of quicksilver were obtained from the mines of Almaden in Spain, Idria in Austria, and Huancavelica in Peru. But of late years quicksilver mines of great abundance have been discovered in California. In a despatch from the Governor of California, published at Washington, in December 1850, he says: "The quicksilver mine of New Almaden, within twelve miles of this place, is valued at several millions of dollars. In a few days they will have twenty-six retorts in operation, and will extract 8000 lbs. daily, worth from 6000 to 8000 dollars—more than 2,000,000 dollars annually. This is only one of the mines, but it is the largest." From these mines considerable quantities of mercury have already been sent to Mexico and South America, and arrangements have been made for opening several silver mines, which before could not be profitably worked. The price of quicksilver, which after the

retain a double standard, if it will go farther in paying our debts in such countries than gold, our silver will disappear let the mint work as hard as it will. The overvalued metal will always drive the undervalued metal out of circulation.

establishment of the independence of the South American States had risen to 130 and even 160 dollars a quintal, has been again reduced to 50 dollars, at which price ore yielding about £13 per ton can be worked with a profit.*

The influence of this discovery in stimulating the production and reducing the value of silver must be very great; and to this and other circumstances affecting the cost of producing silver, we must probably in some degree ascribe the little alteration which has hitherto occurred in the relative value of the two precious metals. For although the price of mercury be an ingredient in the cost of producing gold, it bears an infinitely smaller proportion to the entire value produced than it does in the case of silver. That the present unprecedented importations of gold will by and by lead to the displacement of silver in Europe, as it has already to some extent done in the United States, there can be no doubt. The mode in which such displacements are effected I have considered elsewhere in treating of Exchange.† I shall not resume the subject in this place,

---

* Some Observations on the recent Supplies of Gold, &c., by Andrew Johnson, Bullion Office, Bank of England, pp. 5, 6.

† Philosophy of Trade, book v. chap. ii.

but proceed to examine the laws which determine the value of the precious metals as imported commodities in countries which have no mines of their own,—our observations hitherto having had reference mainly to prices in those countries where gold and silver are produced.

# LETTER XXI.

*Value of the precious metals as imported commodities—
laws which determine their distribution.*

I MUST now return to a subject which I have already
partially explained to you—namely, the distinction between the real and market value of gold and silver.

The value of the metal forming the standard of money
is a different thing altogether from its *price*.  It has in
fact *no price*, and its value is measured by the greater
or smaller quantity of commodities for which a given
portion of the metal will exchange.  All commodities
have a real and a market value—the first dependent on
cost of production, the second upon demand and supply.

Now gold, even when used as the standard of money
and the common measure of value, does not differ from
other commodities in *this* respect—it has a real value,
and it has a market or actual value.  The market value

is sometimes above and sometimes below the real value; but to the real value, as to a fixed point or centre, the market value has a constant tendency to return,—to this, in Adam Smith's language, it gravitates as to a centre of repose and continuance. The real and actual value may never exactly coincide, but the one never diverges from the other without bringing into operation causes by which the deviation is ultimately corrected.

The real value of the material of money, as we have already seen, depends upon the cost of producing the metal, compared with the cost of producing the commodities with which it is exchanged. I take for granted that one metal forms the standard, and that gold is that metal. Given the cost of producing gold, the real value of commodities, estimated in money, or their *price*, will vary directly as the cost of their production, rising as it rises, falling as it falls. Given the cost of producing the commodities, the real value of gold, estimated in such commodities, will vary directly as its cost of production, increasing as it increases, diminishing as it is diminished.

The market, or actual value of gold, depends on the well known principle of demand and supply. Diminish the volume of money in circulation, other things being the same, the market value of money estimated in commodities will rise—in other words, the *price*, or money value, of commodities will fall.   Enlarge the volume of money in circulation, other things being the same, the market value of money estimated in commodities will fall—in other words, the *price* of commodities, or their money value, will rise.

When the market value of money in England, for example, rises above the real value, the metals are attracted to England; for the value of every English commodity being lower in relation to money than to other commodities, other countries can purchase our products more advantageously by the transmission of specie than by the transmission of goods; while we can purchase their commodities cheaper by the transmission of goods than by the transmission of specie.   Money, consequently, continues to flow into England as goods flow out, till the natural level of value in that country is regained.

When, on the other hand, the market value of money in England falls below the real value, the metals begin immediately to flow out of England; for the value of every English commodity being higher in relation to money than to other commodities, other countries can purchase our products more advantageously by the transmission of goods than by the transmission of specie —while we can purchase their productions cheaper by the transmission of specie than by the transmission of goods. Money, consequently, flows out of England as goods flow in, until the natural level of value in that country is restored.

Hence, during the greater portion of the period in which Europe was receiving the vast accessions of the precious metals, consequent on the discovery of the American mines, a stream of metallic wealth, as constant as the trade winds, continued to flow to the east. Humboldt* calculates that of the entire importations, amounting annually at the beginning of the present century to £8,700,000, no less than £5,100,000 were sent to Asia by the Levant, by the Russian Frontier, and by the Cape of Good Hope. As the supplies of the precious metals from America fell off, this easterly current was diminished, and at length ceased altogether. In 1832 and 1833 it set in an opposite direction, till the accessions of gold from the Ural and Siberia again changed it to its former course.

* New Spain, vol. iii. p. 450.

In all discussions regarding the value of the precious metals, we must make due allowance for these fluctuations and disturbances, but the disturbances themselves are subject to known laws, by a knowledge of which we can calculate their magnitude and effect.

The comparative abundance or scarcity of the metals in any country depresses or elevates their market value. But this is not all. You must bear constantly in mind, that in every commercial country there are a thousand expedients for economizing the use of money in the every-day transactions of trade—Bank notes, cheques, credits, bills of exchange, exchequer bills, circular notes, the scrip and share certificates of public companies and undertakings, as banks, railways, canals, docks, even postage stamps are occasionally employed as money; savings banks also tend to economize the use of money, and in the clearing-house of London vast pecuniary transactions, to the amount of from two to three millions daily, are adjusted simply by the exchange of cheques, without the intervention of more than perhaps £200,000 in bank notes, and £20 in specie.

Then you must consider that it is not alone the comparative abundance of money, or its substitutes, that regulates its market value, but the rapidity of its cir-

culation.  In England or the United States, the same
sum of money may change hands four times more frequently than in France, and in France ten times more
frequently than in Russia or Turkey.  Given the
comparative abundance of money, its market value will
vary as the rapidity of circulation.  Given the rapidity
of its circulation, the market value will vary as its comparative abundance.  Given both the quantity and
rapidity, its value will vary as the economy in its use.
When an unfavourable exchange gives unmistakeable
indication of too full a circulation, the nature and extent
of all these disturbing causes must be taken into account
by our bankers, merchants, and statesmen.  But the
political economist especially must never lose sight of
this, that they are mere disturbances, the operation of
which is temporary and self-corrective, and that the
*permanent* value of money depends simply on the cost
of producing the material which composes the standard,
compared with the cost of producing the various commodities to be exchanged.

Now in countries which, having no mines of their
own, import the precious metals from the countries where
they are produced, two elements must be taken into
consideration in estimating this cost—viz. the labour

employed in working up the commodities which are
to be exchanged for the metals, and the labour employed in producing the metals themselves.   We must
take into account the various degrees of efficacy with
which labour is applied to production.   *Ceteris pari-*
*bus*, two days' labour of an Englishman in one department are worth two days' labour of an Englishman in
any other department of industry, and their products
are of equal value.   But two days' labour of an Englishman may be worth three days' labour of a French-
man, or four of a Russian or Pole, or five of a Chinaman
or Hindoo.   We must also take into account the distance of the gold using from the gold producing countries,
and the comparative bulk and *portableness* of the commodities in which the labour of the former is realized.
Hence the average money wages of labour and prices
of commodities vary in different countries.   Hence not
only the market or actual, but the real or cost value
of the precious metals attains a permanently higher
or lower elevation in some of the countries which use
these metals as the materials of their money than
in others; and although in every country the market
value gravitates towards the real value as to a fixed
point, that point may be relatively lower in one country

than in another—lower in Russia or Poland, for example, than in India or China—lower in France
than in Russia or Poland—lower in England than
in France—lower in California and Australia than in
England.

# LETTER XXII.

*Gold and silver as imported commodities—Principle*
*which governs international values.*

THE subject of international values, one of the most
abstruse and difficult which the science of political
economy presents, is very ably discussed (with reference more especially to the precious metals) in an elaborate article in the Edinburgh Review for July 1843.

After demonstrating very clearly that cost of production is the real governor of domestic commerce, the
reviewer goes on to say, " That this is true with respect
to domestic commerce is obvious—it appears to us obvious that it is equally true with respect to international
commerce. The English spinner sells his yarns to the
French importer at precisely the price which he charges
to his English customer. The French weaver sells his
silks to the English importer at precisely the price which

he charges to his French customer. In many cases neither the one nor the other knows for what market he is producing, or to whom he is selling. He produces the quantity for which he expects to get a remunerating price,—a price which will repay the cost of production; that is to say, the cost of the raw material, the interest and wear and tear of his machinery and other fixed capital, the wages of his work-people, and a profit to himself at the current rate of the country, for the time which elapses between his advances and his returns. He sells to a broker, and seldom knows whether his product is to be consumed in England, or America, or France. But it may be said, what is it that decides what shall be the wages of the work-people, which in fact appear to be the positive principle on which price depends, the other elements being mere ratios? Why are the wages of an English cotton spinner four ounces of silver a-week, and those of a French cotton spinner only three? For precisely the same reason that an English cabinetmaker earns 6s. a-day, and an English carpenter only 3s., *the comparative efficiency of their labour*. The produce of the cabinetmaker's day's work is worth a little more than 6s., and therefore he get 6s. The produce of the carpenter's day's work is worth only

a little more than 3s., and therefore he gets 3s.   An
English cotton spinner receives more silver for a day's
work than a French cotton spinner, because he produces
in a day a larger amount of yarn and of a better quality.
The products of the labour and capital of all the French
and all the English manufactures are competitors in the
general market of the world.   The prices at which those
products sell determine the whole sum which is paid for
the result of a given amount of labour of each country,
assisted by a given amount of its capital advanced for
a given time.   The relative proportions in which labour
and capital have concurred in the production, and the
current rate of profit, determine in each country how
much of the price of each commodity is to go to the
labourer, and how much to the capitalist.   If this exceed
average wages or profits, other capitalists or labourers
crowd in; if it be less, the production is in time discon-
tinued.   There is in reality no difference between the
principles which regulate foreign and those which regulate domestic exchanges."*

Now this reasoning appears to be conclusive as far as
it goes, but it does not go far enough.   Assuming the
relative efficiency of French and English labour to be

* Edinburgh Review, vol. lxxviii. pp. 37, 38.

as stated by the reviewer, he has sufficiently accounted
for French wages standing in relation to English wages
in the proportion of 3 to 4, or of 15 to 20, or of 75 to 100.
But then we want to get at the root of the matter.  We
want to know not only why the English cotton spinner
gets an ounce of silver more for his week's work than
the French cotton spinner, but why he gets neither
more nor less than four ounces?  True, the cost of four
ounces of silver in England is just the cost of producing
the cotton cloth which is the result of a week's work.
If this quantity of cloth comes to cost less than a week's
work, things in France and in the country of the mines
being the same, English wages will rise—if it comes to
cost more, English wages will fall; they will fall in relation to French wages.  But in the actual circumstances
assumed by the reviewer, we want to be informed why
English wages amount to four ounces of silver, and why
French wages amount to three ounces?  In short, we
want to know the laws which determine the proportions
in which the products of European labour—and European labour itself—will exchange for the silver of
Mexico or the gold of Australia?

Mr J. S. Mill has essayed the solution of this difficult
problem, but as far as I can see without complete suc-

cess.  After all the attention I can give to his very acute and able reasoning, I must say he appears to me to have failed in explaining the laws by which these proportions are determined, and he has failed, it would seem, from having assumed originally too narrow an hypothesis as the basis of his argument.  It is fair to give the conclusion at which he arrives in his own words.  " It may be considered," he says, " as established, that when two countries trade together in two commodities, the exchange value of these commodities relatively to each other will adjust itself to the inclinations and circumstances of the consumers on both sides, in such manner that the quantities required by each country of the articles which it imports from its neighbour shall be exactly sufficient to pay for one another.  As the inclinations and circumstances of consumers cannot be reduced to any rule, so neither can the proportions in which the two commodities will be interchanged.  We know that the limits within which the variation is confined are the ratio between their costs of production in the one country, and the ratio between their costs of production in the other."*

The case stated and reasoned upon by Mr Mill is

* Principles of Political Economy, vol. ii. p. 126.

that of an interchange of two commodities between two
countries, but he holds that "trade among any number
of countries and in any number of commodities must
take place on the same essential principles as trade between two countries and in two commodities."* Now,
I have already shown,† that without assuming the existence of some *third* commodity as a standard, we have
no means of comparing values, and without such a
standard the proportions in which the two commodities
will exchange for each other can be determined only
by the higgling of the market. But here we have a
third subject of exchange—cost of production—be it
labour, capital, or what it will. Were human labour
as readily transferable from one country to another as
silver or cochineal, international values would be determined on the same principle as domestic values. In
that case, if more silver could be got by the direct
application of labour to mining than to the production
of those commodities with which silver is purchased,
labour would be instantly transferred from the one department to the other, and values would be equalized
between England and Mexico in the same way as they

* Principles of Political Economy, vol. ii. p. 128.
† *Ante*, Letter I.

are equalized between Yorkshire and Lancashire. But man, as Adam Smith says, is of all luggage the most difficult to transport. Differences of laws, of language, of manners, and modes of living, the love of home, domestic ties, early associations, and a thousand circumstances, are bars to the easy transfer of human labour from one country to another. But although labour itself is with difficulty transferred, no such difficulty attends the transfer of the products of labour. We must take one or other of these products, therefore, and not labour, as our standard of comparison, and then (as I shall endeavour to demonstrate in my next letter) the problem can be resolved on the basis of cost of production alone; and although we cannot discard the consideration of demand and supply in either case, international will be placed on the same footing as domestic exchanges.

" Does the law that permanent value is proportioned to cost of production hold good between commodities produced in distant places, as it does between those produced in adjacent places?" asks Mr Mill, and he answers, " That it does not."*

Again,† he says, " The value of a commodity brought

* Principles of Political Economy, vol. ii. p. 110.	† Ib. p. 121.

from a distant place, especially from a foreign country, does not depend on its cost of production in the place from whence it comes. On what then does it depend? The value of a thing in any place depends on the cost of its acquisition in that place; which, in the case of an imported article, means the cost of production of the thing which is exported to pay for it." As regards value there can be no doubt that this statement is quite correct; but what we are now discussing is the *problem of proportions.* If for 100 bales of cloth I get at one time 50 pipes of wine, and at another 100, the 100 pipes in the one case will be of the same *value* in the importing country as the 50 pipes in the other; but the proportions in which the two commodities exchange for each other are of course very different. The proportions depend upon the cost at home and the cost abroad, upon what I give and upon what I get, and both must be taken into account.

Mr Mill makes the supposition that ten yards of broad cloth cost in England as much labour as fifteen yards of linen, and in Germany as much as twenty. "This supposition being made, it would be the interest of England to import linen from Germany, and of Germany to import cloth from England. When each country produced both commodities for itself, ten yards of cloth exchanged for fifteen yards of linen in England, and for twenty in Germany. They will now exchange for the same number of yards of linen in both. For what number? If for fifteen yards, England will be just as she was, and Germany will gain all. If for twenty yards, Germany will be as before, and England will derive the whole of the benefit. If for any number intermediate between fifteen and twenty, the advantage will be shared between the two countries. If, for example, ten yards of cloth exchange for eighteen of linen, England will gain an advantage of three yards on every fifteen, Germany will save two out of every twenty. The problem is, *What are the causes which determine the proportion in which the cloth of England and the linen of Germany will exchange for each other?*"* After much ingenious reasoning upon these premises, Mr Mill arrives at the following solution of the problem: " Ten yards of cloth cannot exchange for more than twenty yards of linen, nor for less than fifteen. But they may exchange for any intermediate number. The ratios, therefore, in which the advantage of the trade may be divided between the two nations are various. The

* Principles of Political Economy, vol. ii. pp. 123, 124.

circumstances on which the proportionate share of each country more remotely depends, admit only of a very general indication."* In short, the proportions depend upon a law which he terms the Equation of International Demand, and which, within the limits of the cost of production on both sides, would appear to differ little if at all from Adam Smith's principle of supply and demand.

To test the value of this theory, let us put the case somewhat differently. Suppose that in England twenty yards of cloth and ten yards of linen are the produce of the same amount of labour and capital, which in Germany produce twenty yards of linen and ten yards of cloth. In these circumstances, England, by sending twenty yards of cloth to Germany, would, at the German par of value,† obtain in exchange forty yards of linen, or Germany, by sending twenty yards of linen to England, would, at the English par, obtain in exchange forty yards of cloth. In either case the advantage would be all on one side. On Mr Mill's principles, we should probably solve the problem correctly by saying that

* Principles of Political Economy, vol. ii. p. 126.

† *Par of value* I use to denote the products of equal capitals or an equal amount of labour.

twenty yards of English cloth could not exchange for more than forty yards of German linen, nor for less than ten, and that the exact proportions would depend upon the equation of international demand, in other words, upon the inclinations and circumstances of the consumers of cloth and linen.  This is no doubt an extreme case, but it is just by supposing such extreme cases that the truth and value of a theory are to be tested.

The conclusion arrived at by Mr Mill is fairly enough deduced from his assumed premises, but his premises are too narrow to afford a satisfactory solution of the problem.*  On the hypothesis of an interchange of only

---

* The same observation appears to apply to the following case put by Mr James Mill, in his *Elements of Political Economy* (2d edit., p. 115), " If the cloth and the corn, each of which required 100 days' labour in Poland, required each 150 days' labour in England, it would follow that the cloth of 150 days' labour in England, if sent to Poland, would be equal to the cloth of 100 days' labour in Poland.  If exchanged for corn, therefore, it would exchange for the corn of only 100 days' labour.  But the corn of 100 days' labour in Poland was supposed to be the same quantity with that of 150 days' labour in England.  With 150 days' labour in cloth, therefore, England would only get as much corn in Poland as she could raise with 150 days' labour at home ; and she would on importing it have the cost of carriage besides. *In these circumstances no exchange would take place.*"  Now this

*two* commodities without reference to capital, or any third commodity or subject of exchange, the problem is insoluble: there is *no* principle upon which we can determine the proportions; and England and Germany in the circumstances supposed would exchange broad cloth and linen just as Captain Cook exchanged beads and looking-glasses against the products of the South Sea Islands. The proportions would be determined, not by any exact rule, but according to that sort of rough equality which results from the higgling of the market. The labour of each country, in the case supposed, is the only standard of comparison that I can imagine between the value of the two commodities, and labour by the hypothesis cannot be transferred, or, what

conclusion is logically deduced from the premises, but the premises are too narrow. Here we have *two* commodities, corn and cloth—the *third* subject of exchange being *labour*, by hypothesis not transferable. For *labour* substitute *capital*, and you will see at once that an exchange *would* take place. If, by employing a capital equal to 100, as much corn and cloth can be produced in another country as I can produce in this country by employing one equal to 150, that capital will not be employed here in the production of these two commodities, but will be either directly sent abroad, or worked up into another commodity which will be sent abroad, and exchanged for one-third more corn and cloth than can be produced by it at home.

comes practically to the same thing, seldom or never is transferred.    Substitute capital,—or silver or any other representative of capital, readily transferable from the one country to the other, and you will see at once that, under the circumstances we have supposed (we lay aside for the present the consideration of cost of carriage, insurance, taxes, &c., which would only render the case more complex without affecting the conclusion), the cloth of England would exchange for the linen of Germany in the proportion of twenty yards of the one for twenty yards of the other, and that each country would thus participate equally in the benefits of the trade. No man in England would give more than twenty yards of cloth for twenty yards of linen, when by sending the capital which produced the cloth to Germany he could procure that number of yards.    No man in Germany would take less than twenty yards of cloth for twenty yards of linen, when by sending the capital which produced the linen to England he could procure that quantity of the other commodity.    Cost, then, would seem to govern international as it does domestic exchanges. The market price may temporarily exceed or fall short of the natural price, but to this, after a longer or shorter interval, it invariably returns.

# LETTER XXIII.

### *Principle of international values.*

I HAVE already intimated that the permanent value of gold and silver, as determined by cost of production—the real or natural value to which the market value conforms—is higher in some countries which import these metals as the materials of their money, than in others.

Let us now examine the laws which determine the proportions in which the precious metals and the exported commodities wherewith they are purchased will exchange for each other, and also the laws which determine the money price of labour in each country. The inquiry is abstruse and complicated in no ordinary degree, and I must claim for the subject of this and the following letter your earnest and undivided attention.

Suppose two countries—England and Mexico—and

that the following are the products of a thousand days'
labour in each country respectively, viz. :—

|  | England. | Mexico. |  |
|---|---|---|---|
| 1000 days' labour = | 50 tons iron. 25 cwt. tin. 50 qrs. wheat. 150 yds. cloth. | 50 tons iron, 400 oz. silver, 100 qrs. wheat, 75 yds. cloth, | = 1000 days' labour. |

Let the commodities in the production of which the
labour of England is the more efficient be represented
by *cloth;* those in which Mexican labour is the more
efficient by *corn;* and those in which the labour of
both countries is equally efficient by *iron;* while *tin*
represents commodities peculiar to England, and *silver*
commodities peculiar to Mexico. I omit, as before,
the consideration of cost of carriage, &c., and, for the
sake of illustration, I assume silver to be the sole standard of money at the rate of 5s. per ounce.

Now, Mexico wishes to exchange her corn against
English cloth. In what proportions will these two commodities, in the hypothetical circumstances I have stated,
exchange for one another? In England, 50 quarters of
wheat and 150 yards of cloth are equivalents, for they
are each the product of an equal amount of labour.
But England will not give 150 yards of cloth for 50
quarters of wheat, when by sending 50 tons of iron,

by supposition also the equivalent of 150 yards of cloth, she can obtain 100 quarters of wheat in the Mexican market. England will not consent to give 150 yards of her cloth for less than 100 quarters.

On the other hand, suppose England had desired to exchange her cloth against Mexican corn, at the Mexican par of 75 yards of cloth for 100 quarters of wheat, or, what is the .same thing, 150 yards for 200 quarters, Mexico would not submit to make the exchange in these proportions, because by exporting iron she can procure cloth at the English par of 150 yards for 50 tons; and 50 tons of iron are by hypothesis the equivalent in Mexico of 100 quarters.

The rate of exchange, the proportions, will therefore be, as before, 150 yards = 100 quarters. For each country can command the market of the other through those commodities (represented in our supposed case by iron), in which the efficiency of their labour is equal. The labour cannot readily be transferred, but its products can.

But if the efficiency of the labour of either country in the production of these last commodities be relatively increased (in other words, if the cost of production in either country be relatively diminished), the country of

superior efficiency, or inferior cost, will gain a corresponding advantage in all her exchanges with the country
whose efficiency remains as before.   To test this, change
the hypothesis somewhat, and suppose the case to stand
thus :—

|  | England. | | Mexico. | |
|---|---|---|---|---|
| 1000 days' labour = | 55 tons iron.<br>25 cwt. tin.<br>50 qrs. wheat.<br>150 yds. cloth. | | 50 tons iron,<br>400 oz. silver,<br>100 qrs. wheat,<br>75 yds. cloth, | = 1000 days' labour. |

Mexico now wishes to exchange her corn against
English cloth at the former rate of 100 quarters for
150 yards.   In England, 50 quarters and 150 yards
are still equivalents, but 55 tons of iron (instead of 50)
are now the equivalent of 150 yards of cloth.   England
can now, therefore, in exchange for 150 yards of cloth,
obtain 110 quarters of wheat, in place of 100 quarters
as formerly.   For that reason, England will not consent
to give the equivalent of 55 tons of iron (150 yards of
cloth) for less than 110 quarters.

Nor can Mexico now force the exchange on more
favourable terms to herself.   The reason, observe, why
Mexico formerly refused to exchange corn for cloth at
her own par of 75 yards=100 quarters, was, that by
exporting iron (in the production of which her own

labour and that of England were then equally efficient),
she could produce for the equivalent of 100 quarters
(50 tons of iron) 150 yards of cloth. But *now* that
power is taken away by the superior efficiency of English
labour in the production of iron, or that class of
commodities which iron is supposed to represent. In
the altered circumstances supposed, by exporting 50
tons of iron to England, Mexico can obtain little more
than 135 yards of cloth. To procure the former quantity
of 150 yards, Mexico must now, therefore, give 55 tons
of iron, the equivalent at the Mexican par not of 100,
but of 110 quarters of wheat. It is therefore a matter
of indifference to the Mexican exporter whether he give
55 tons of iron or 110 quarters of wheat; and the proportions will, therefore, in this altered state of things,
be 150 yards of English cloth for 110 quarters of
Mexican wheat.

Of course it is the interest of each country to exchange
the commodities in the production of which she most
excels—in the production of which her labour and capital are relatively most efficient—at the par of the country
which excels less in the production of the same commodities; and not at her own par. It is the interest of
England, for example, in the case first put, to exchange

her cloth against the corn of Mexico at the Mexican par of 150 yards=200 quarters. But then it is equally the interest of the Mexican exporter to frustrate this attempt to appropriate his produce at so much less an expense of labour and capital than it cost himself; and for this purpose he selects for exportation that commodity in the production of which the labour and capital of both countries is equally efficient, *or most nearly so.* If equal quantities of iron are the products of equal labour in both countries, Mexico obtains 150 yards of cloth at exactly the same expense of labour which the production of that cloth cost England; while had Mexico paid for it in corn at the English par (50 quarters=150 yards), it would have cost her double that amount of labour.

In the case first supposed, Mexico gives 50 tons of iron for 150 yards of cloth. But after the efficiency of English labour has increased by 10 per cent., it is still the interest of Mexico to select iron as the commodity to export in exchange for English cloth. Mexico, it is true, cannot now obtain the cloth at the same expense of labour which it costs England, for English labour in the production of that commodity is more efficient by one-tenth; but still iron, in the language of trade, is

the *best remittance;* for although the labour of both
countries is not now equally efficient in the production
of that commodity, it is more nearly equal than in the
production of any other.   Mexico, to obtain 150 yards
of English cloth, must now give 55 tons of iron, or 440
ounces of silver,—the products of 1100 days' Mexican
labour, in exchange for the products of 1000 days' English labour.   The terms of the exchange are regulated
by the relative efficiency of the labour of the two countries in the production, not of all commodities, but of
those commodities in the production of which their efficiency is most nearly equal.

Having thus demonstrated the effect of the increased
efficiency of English labour in the production of that
class of commodities symbolized by *iron* in the original
formula, let us examine the effect which would be
produced by increased efficiency on either side in the
production of commodities *peculiar* to either country,
represented by silver in Mexico and by tin in England.

1. Suppose that our labour in the production of tin
is doubled in efficiency, all things else remaining as
before; thus,

|  | England. |  | Mexico. |  |
|---|---|---|---|---|
| 1000 days' labour = | 50 tons iron. 50 cwt. tin. 50 qrs. wheat. 150 yds. cloth. | | 50 tons iron, 400 oz. silver, 100 qrs. wheat, 75 yds. cloth, | = 1000 days' labour. |

We here suppose the quantity of tin produced in England by 1000 days' labour to be 50 instead of 25 cwt. Formerly 25 cwt. of tin being the equivalent of 50 tons of iron in England, and 50 tons of iron being the equivalent of 400 ounces of silver in Mexico, the price or money value of tin (taking silver at 5s. per ounce) was 80s. per cwt. After the change in the efficiency of English labour, and in consequence of it, the price of tin, and its value in relation to all commodities, both at home and abroad, will fall by one-half, the price will sink to 40s. per cwt., but no change will take place in the price or value of labour, or of any other commodity.

2. Suppose, again, the efficiency of mining labour in Mexico to be doubled, all things else remaining as before; thus,

|  | England. |  | Mexico. |  |
|---|---|---|---|---|
| 1000 days' labour = | 50 tons iron. 25 cwt. tin. 50 qrs. wheat. 150 yds. cloth. | | 50 tons iron, 800 oz. silver, 100 qrs. wheat, 75 yds. cloth, | = 1000 days' labour. |

Here we suppose the quantity of silver produced by 1000 days' Mexican labour to be 800 ounces, instead of 400 ounces as before. The consequence of this, upon the principles before stated, must be that the value of silver will sink by one-half, or, in other words, that the money prices of all things will be doubled. Formerly, 400 ounces of silver being the equivalent of 50 tons of iron in Mexico, and 50 tons of iron in England being the equivalent of 25 cwt. of tin, 150 yards of cloth, &c., 400 ounces could be obtained in exchange for those quantities of either commodity, in other words, the price of tin was 80s. per cwt., and of English cloth 13s. 4d. a-yard. After the change of the efficiency of mining labour, and in consequence of it, the value of silver in relation to labour and to all commodities, whether in Mexico or England, will fall one-half. 800 instead of 400 ounces of silver are now the equivalent of 1000 days' labour, 50 tons iron, 150 yards of cloth, &c.; money wages, therefore, will be doubled in Mexico and all other countries, and the price of commodities will be doubled; tin will now sell for 160s. a-cwt., English cloth for 26s. 8d. a-yard, &c. But the change being peculiar to silver, all other commodities will continue of the same value each to each, and although money wages are doubled, real wages will undergo no change.  The labourer with double the amount of silver can command no more corn, cloth, &c., than he could before the change.

I shall conclude this abstruse, and I fear very forbidding, subject in my next letter.

# LETTER XXIV.

*Principle of international values.*

WE have seen that when an increased quantity of any commodity is produced by a given amount of labour, in other words, when labour in any one department becomes more efficient, the value of that commodity in relation to gold, silver, and other commodities produced under the same conditions as formerly, falls—it falls in relation to commodities produced in the same country, and it also falls in relation to foreign commodities to the full extent of the diminution in its cost, provided there be no change in the cost of another class of commodities, in the production of which the labour of the exporting and importing countries are equally efficient, or more nearly so, than in the production of the commodity which has undergone the change. In the hypothetical case stated in my last letter for the purpose of

illustration, I supposed *iron* to represent those commodities in the production of which the labour of England
and Mexico was equally efficient, or most nearly so—
and from which consequently what I would call the
*par of international value* must be deduced.  Let us now
carry the illustration farther, and suppose the efficiency
of English labour to be increased 10 per cent. in the
production not only of that class of commodities represented by iron, but of all commodities, the efficiency of
Mexican labour remaining as formerly, thus :—

|  | *England.* |  | *Mexico.* |  |
|---|---|---|---|---|
| 1000 days' labour = | ⎧ 55 tons iron. ⎪ 27½ cwt. tin. ⎨ 55 qrs. wheat. ⎩ 165 yds. cloth. | ⎪ | 50 tons iron, 400 oz. silver, 100 qrs. wheat, 75 yds. cloth, | ⎫ ⎪ ⎬ = 1000 days' ⎪ labour. ⎭ |

Were the efficiency of English labour thus increased
in the production of *all* commodities, and increased in
equal proportion, no change whatever would take place
in the ratios of exchange with Mexico.  For 400 ounces
of silver being the equivalent in Mexico of 50 tons of
iron, and 55 tons of iron being the equivalent in England of 165 yards of cloth, 400 ounces of silver would
purchase no more than 150 yards of cloth.  To test
this, suppose Mexico to send 50 tons of iron to the
English market,—at our par 50 tons of iron are the

equivalent of 150 yards of cloth; and if England send 55 tons of iron to Mexico, that quantity will exchange at the Mexican par for 440 ounces of silver, equal to 165 yards of cloth at 13s. 4d. a-yard, which was the price of cloth before the change. No alteration will take place in the proportions in which commodities will exchange either at home or abroad, and no alteration of values or prices. But an important change will be caused in the price and value of English *labour*. Money wages and real wages will rise by 10 per cent. Observe how the case now stands: England *for the products of the same amount of labour* (1000 days), viz. 55 tons of iron, 165 yards of cloth, &c., will now obtain one-tenth more of every Mexican commodity. England will now obtain for the results of her 1000 days' labour 440 oz. of silver, 110 quarters of wheat, &c. The products will still bear to each other the old proportions, but they will bear an altered proportion to the labour which produced them. Money wages will be raised 10 per cent., because 1000 days' labour expended in the manufacture of English commodities will now obtain 440 ounces of silver, instead of 400. Real wages will rise 10 per cent., because 1000 days' labour in the manufacture of English commodities is more efficient by one-tenth, and the products of a day's labour will exchange for one-tenth more of the products of Mexico, and all other countries.

The case would have been different if the increased efficiency had not been universal or in equal proportion. If the labour employed in producing iron, or the class of commodities which iron is supposed to represent, had alone risen in efficiency by 10 per cent., without any corresponding change in Mexico, not only would the price and value of English labour have risen 10 per cent., but the price and value of all commodities produced under the former conditions.

Had our efficiency in these last commodities also increased, but increased to the extent of 5 per cent. only, their prices and values would likewise have risen, but the effect would have been modified in a corresponding degree.

Of course I must be understood here to speak, not of accidental and temporary but of permanent international values, and as by no means undervaluing the principle of supply and demand, by the agency of which commodities, when they happen for a time to deviate from the par of international value, are ultimately brought back to par. The Mexican market may, for instance, be temporarily overstocked with corn, in which case a larger proportional quantity of corn will exchange for given quantities of iron, cloth, and other English products; or the English market may be overstocked with iron, in which case a larger proportional quantity of iron will exchange for a given quantity of silver and other Mexican products. But such deviation from the international par of value cannot occur without bringing into operation a principle by which the divergence will be ultimately corrected. The tendency is still towards the par as a centre; and the par must be deduced from those commodities whereof equal quantities in both countries most nearly represent equal quantities of labour.

Suppose that, from a temporary superabundance of corn in Mexico, the value of that commodity, in relation to iron, silver, and other products, is diminished. Suppose that, instead of 100 quarters of wheat exchanging as formerly for 50 tons of iron in Mexico, 200 quarters exchange for 50 tons. It now becomes the interest of Mexico to send corn rather than iron to purchase cloth in the English market, and it is equally the interest of England to import corn at its reduced value. More and more corn will thus be exported from Mexico and imported into England—the value of corn, in relation to iron, cloth, and other commodities, will in consequence fall in England, and rise in Mexico.  More and more corn will be given in England for 50 tons of iron, and less and less in Mexico.  But when in England, by the action of these causes, 150 quarters of wheat come to exchange for 50 tons of iron, and in Mexico 150 quarters also come to exchange for 50 tons, it becomes a matter of pure indifference to the Mexican merchant whether he export corn or iron in exchange for cloth, and to the English merchant whether he import the one commodity or the other.  But when again, by the continued action of the same causes, the value of corn in relation to iron, &c., in England, falls below this point, when these commodities exchange, for instance, in the proportion of 160 quarters for 50 tons in England, and in the proportion of 140 quarters for 50 tons in Mexico —it then becomes the interest of Mexico to pay for Engglish cloth, not in corn, but in iron.  The value of corn in both countries will continue lower than formerly till the temporary superabundance is relieved; but the value of cloth, in relation to iron, silver, and all other commodities, both in Mexico and in England, will at length be restored to the original par.

Reviewing the argument of this and the preceding letter, we appear now to have arrived at the following general conclusions :—

1. The cause which determines the proportions in which the commodities of two countries will exchange for each other is the comparative efficiency of the labour of such countries—or, to use an equivalent expression, the comparative cost of production.

2. The greater the relative efficiency of the labour of any country, the more of every foreign commodity will a determinate portion of the produce of such country exchange for.

3. A general increase of the relative efficiency of labour in all departments, if in equal proportion, will raise the money price of labour in the same way as the increased productiveness of the mines, and also its real value in relation to commodities both foreign and domestic, but it will have no effect upon the price and value of commodities themselves.

4. An increase of the relative efficiency of labour, not general, but confined to those commodities in the production of which both countries have most nearly equal facilities, will raise the price and value of labour in the country whose efficiency has increased, and also the

price and value of all its commodities, except those in the production of which the efficiency of the two countries is most nearly equal. If the increased relative efficiency of labour extend to other commodities, but in a less degree, their prices will also rise, but the effect will be proportionally modified.

5. Were the labour of both countries increased in efficiency and increased universally, and in equal proportion, no effect would be produced on the values and prices of commodities. Double the quantity of produce on all sides; thus,

|  | *England.* |  | *Mexico.* |  |
|---|---|---|---|---|
| 1000 days' labour = | 100 tons iron. 50 cwt. tin. 100 qrs. wheat. 300 yds. cloth. | | 100 tons iron, 800 oz. silver, 200 qrs. wheat, 150 yds. cloth, | = 1000 days' labour. |

The same quantity of each commodity will, after the change here supposed, still exchange for the former quantity of each, and of money. Not so with the wages of labour. The amount of labour on both sides remaining as before, and the mines having doubled their productiveness, money wages will rise 100 per cent. both in Mexico and in England, and real wages (or the value of labour estimated in commodities) will rise in the same proportion. For money wages being doubled, and the

prices of all commodities remaining as before, the labourer, after the change, and in consequence of it, can
command double the former quantity of every thing he
wishes to consume.

I shall not attempt to pursue this subject through all
its ramifications, which would occupy a volume.   My
object is simply to explain to you the principle which
determines the permanent value of gold and silver as
money, in countries which, having no mines of their
own, obtain these metals in exchange for their products,
and that object, I trust, I have now sufficiently accomplished.

# LETTER XXV.

*Probable consequences of the gold discoveries—the revenue
—Public debt—Fixed incomes—Poor-rates.*

HAVING said so much upon the laws which determine
the value of the precious metals, and their distribution
among the different countries of the world, and having
ventured to indicate an opinion upon a still more difficult subject—namely, the *time* when that change in the
relative value of money and commodities, which now
appears to be inevitable, may be expected to take place
—the next subject which demands our attention is the
effect which that change is likely to produce upon the
condition of the various classes of society.

My deliberate conviction is, that if the present rate of
production is continued but for a very few years longer,
a great mercantile and social change may be expected
—a disturbance of the existing relations of property

such as the world has not seen for nearly three centuries; and that we shall deceive ourselves by a false
analogy if we conclude that the flood of gold which is
now pouring in upon our markets from Russia, from
California, and from Australia, added to unabated supplies from older sources, will be as tardy in its operation
upon prices as the increased supply of silver was in
former days.

The conditions under which the two metals are produced, as I have endeavoured to prove to you, are totally different.  Golden Potosis (if I may be allowed the
expression) have been already discovered, and are yielding up their treasures to Anglo-Saxon industry, unaided
by expensive appliances and complicated machinery.
Without waiting for the advent of another Velasco, the
discovery of a second Huancavelica, and the introduction of new chemical and metallurgical processes, we
are already receiving additions to our metallic wealth
unparalleled in the history of the world, and at a reduction of cost equally unprecedented.

As yet no very perceptible effect has been produced
upon general prices, except in Australia and America,
the countries of the mines, and little or no alteration
has taken place in the relative value of the precious

metals themselves. Now, therefore, is the time for us to sit down and examine deliberately the consequences which the maintenance of a gold standard is likely to entail upon agriculture, upon commerce, upon manufactures, upon government, upon the condition of our labourers and artisans, and the material prosperity of all ranks and classes of the community.

In Holland, silver has already been adopted as the sole standard of money, for the purpose of eluding the effects of the coming changes. With us, the general voice would appear to be loud and decided in favour of adhering at all hazards to our existing measure of value, —a determination to which no exception can be taken on the score of equity and justice, however great the suffering which it may entail upon individuals and classes. But since it is so, it behoves us now to count the cost and reckon up the consequences. If we are to encounter difficulties, let us look them steadily in the face, and learn accurately beforehand their nature and extent.

By maintaining gold as our standard, no doubt, the dead-weight of the enormous public debt under which England has so long groaned will be materially lightened; but let it not be forgotten that the burden will not be removed. It will merely be shifted to other shoulders—shoulders much less able to bear the incubus than those upon which it now so uneasily presses. It is a mistake to talk of the "Fundholders" in the gross, as if they were a congregation of *Millionaires*, a set of men of overgrown fortune, living in wealth and ease, and fit subjects for a public experiment. It really is not so. An authentic voucher proves, that of the 282,349 persons to whom quarterly dividends were paid in October 1841 and January 1842, 85,991 held sums which produced dividends of less amount than £5; 45,396 received less than £10; 100,144 less than £50; 26,604 less than £100.*

Now, should those changes, on the effects of which we have been speculating, actually take place, and reduce money to one-third of its present value,† should

* M'Culloch's Commercial Dictionary—Art. *Funds.*

† I need not say that I make this assumption at random, and merely for the purpose of illustration. No human being can as yet venture to estimate the *degree* of effect likely to be produced by the recent gold discoveries, although the *kind* of effect may be predicted with some measure of certainty. Practically, there can be no doubt that as the number of gold diggers is enlarged,— while the supplies of the metal on the whole will be greatly augmented,—the average earnings of each labourer will be sensibly diminished, and the cost of producing the metal consequently increased; while on the other hand,—with the impetus given by

the prices of all things be tripled or quadrupled, as they were in the sixteenth century, these persons—including tens of thousands of feeble old men, aged mothers, unprotected sisters, widows, orphans, charitable and provident institutions, and those dependant on them —must sustain the weight, of which our landowners, merchants, and manufacturers are relieved. True, the nominal amount of dividends which these parties now receive will not be reduced; but the value of the dividends will be materially diminished. Wealth, be it remembered, although reckoned in gold and silver,

recent legislation to commerce in all its branches, the opening up of new markets, and new and more rapid means of conveyance, unrestricted competition, useful inventions and discoveries, the progressive advancement of science, and improvements in the mechanical arts,—the cost of producing the commodities which are to be exchanged for the precious metals will be concurrently reduced. These causes, with the time necessary for the inter- mediate displacement of silver, will go far to modify, or re- tard, the effects of the gold discoveries on general prices. Still there is serious reason to apprehend an alarming disturbance of the existing equilibrium; and with the writer of an article in the *Times* (of 25th June last), which has deservedly attracted much attention, I can arrive at no other conclusion than that "the Australian and Californian discoveries, even at their present rate of yield, will produce effects of a momentous character, which nothing is likely in any material manner to counteract."

does not consist in these metals. "The great wheel of circulation," says Adam Smith, "is altogether different from the goods which are circulated by means of it, and every man is rich or poor, not according to the number of white or yellow pieces of metal which he has in his pocket, but according as he can afford to enjoy the necessaries, conveniences, and amusements of human life."*

The man who has invested £100 in 3 per cent. stock will still receive £3 a-year; but that sum, which at present prices commands 120 quartern loaves, will, after the change we have supposed, purchase perhaps only 40, and every thing else will rise in the same proportion. No doubt had this person not invested his £100 in consols, but retained it in his own possession, the principal would have been proportionally as much reduced in value as the interest. Government when it borrowed his money did not do more than engage to pay him a fixed annuity of £3 a-year, or as much gold of our present standard as that sum contains, or else to pay him back the principal, or gold equal to 100 pounds. This in law, and perhaps in strict equity and justice,

* Wealth of Nations, book i. chap. v.

must be accepted as a sufficient answer—an answer to which, as far as I can see, there is no legitimate rejoinder. Any argument which the fundholders can employ must resolve itself very much into an *argumentum ad misericordiam*, to which, it is to be feared, little attention will or can be paid. But let the classes who have the prospect of benefiting by the change rejoice with trembling. We may not have to struggle through more than a quarter of a century of public and domestic suffering, as our ancestors had after the last great revolution in the value of the precious metals; but neither can we expect a shock of such magnitude, affecting such vital interests, and involving the impoverishment of so many families, to pass over without being acutely felt in every joint and member of the body politic. Let us glance at the interests which are mainly to suffer, and then at those which are likely to profit by the change.

To begin with the public—the government—our present burdens may be stated in round numbers at fifty millions per annum, of which thirty millions go to pay the interest of our debt, and the remaining twenty to defray the current expenses of the state. No change in the value of money will directly affect the interest of the debt, but, were the prices of commodities generally raised threefold, as they were in Queen Elizabeth's reign, it is quite clear that the twenty millions for the current expenditure must be tripled.  The pay of soldiers and sailors, of civil servants, judges, public officers, and functionaries, the prices of naval and military stores, ships, and munitions of war, all must be raised threefold.  While the interest of our debt would be no greater than at present, the twenty millions for the current requirements of the public service must probably be increased to sixty millions.  The ability of the producing classes to pay taxes would be increased threefold; but let us not forget that the taxes themselves must in that case be also largely increased.

Look at the struggles to which a similar necessity for raising additional taxes to meet the enhanced price of labour and commodities gave rise in the reigns of James the First and his unhappy son.  Great principles were then at stake, no doubt;—interests of far mightier concernment than those which involve mere fiscal and financial considerations were in jeopardy;—but we are not for that reason hastily to conclude that an unreasoning impatience of taxation in the mind of the nation at large—impatience of increasing exactions, rendered necessary by the depreciated value of money, a matter then little understood—had no share in engendering the discontents and inflaming the animosities and contentions of that calamitous period. Let us advert for a moment to the state of the public revenue from 1574, when the first marked rise of prices in Europe took place, till 1650, when, according to Baron Humboldt, it appears to have reached its utmost limit.

The revenue of England, which in Elizabeth's reign did not exceed £500,000 a-year, that great queen, notwithstanding the wise economy which she practised, was obliged to eke out by dilapidating the royal demesnes, and this alone saved her from applying to parliament for additional supplies.* The revenue of James I. amounted to £450,000, of which the crown lands yielded £80,000, but it fell short of his disbursements by £36,000 a-year. The extraordinary sums raised during his reign by loans, subsidies, sale of lands and of the title of baronet, benevolences, money received from the French king, &c., amounted to £2,200,000, of which £775,000 was from the sale of crown lands. This monarch was consequently involved in debt, and

* Hume's History of England, App. iii.

with all his expedients had great difficulty in supporting his government.* From 1637 until the meeting of the Long Parliament, Charles's revenue was £900,000, of which he levied £200,000 illegally. From 1649 to 1660, the taxes amounted to about £2,000,000 a-year; but Cromwell died two millions in debt. During the protectorship of Richard Cromwell, the whole public revenue amounted to £1,868,717, while his expenses were £2,201,540.† Thus we see that during the whole period which intervened between the middle of Elizabeth's reign, when the importations of the metals from America began to produce their effect upon prices, down to the Restoration, successive governments had to struggle with inadequate revenues, and a constantly increasing expenditure. England, in fact, for more than a quarter of a century, resembled a patient writhing under a mysterious organic disease, ascribing her sufferings to everything but the true cause. Similar financial difficulties may again occur. The same causes are at work, and may be followed by the same effects. It is our wisdom, therefore, to be prepared. If general prices advance, taxes must advance along with them.

* Hume's History of England, App. to reign of James I.
† Ib. chap. 62.

Our landlords, merchants, and manufacturers may, in the heyday of rising prices and increasing rents and profits, submit with cheerfulness to the constantly increasing exactions of the Chancellor of the Exchequer; but from dowagers, annuitants, pensioners, fundholders, mortgagees, and all that class whose fixed money incomes will be cut down, or, what is the same thing, reduced permanently in purchasing power, we must be prepared for a long-continued cry of suffering and distress.

Our paupers, too, are a class of annuitants who will join in the cry. The general enhancement of prices which took place in Elizabeth's reign had perhaps as much to do with the introduction of poor rates as the cause to which it is more usually ascribed—namely, the dissolution of the monasteries in the preceding reign. In 1563, the first compulsory provision was made for the maintenance of the poor—followed in 1572 by a statute authorizing parochial assessments—and ultimately by the well known 43d of Elizabeth, which established the vicious system which prevailed down to a comparatively recent period.*

* Compare these *dates* with those given *ante*, Letter XIV., pp. 132—136.

Nor was the next general rise of prices which took place after the middle of the eighteenth century un-attended with an increase of pauperism. " So recently as the reign of George II., the amount raised within the year for poor rates and county rates in England and Wales was only £730,000. This was the average amount collected in 1748–49–50. In 1775, the amount was more than doubled, having been £1,750,000, of which sum rather more than a million and a half was expended for the relief of the poor."*

Similar effects followed the great fall in the value of money which was consequent on the suspension of cash payments by the Bank of England, and the over-issues of inconvertible paper. The annual sum expended for the relief of the poor continued to increase, till for the three years from 1812–13 to 1814–15 the average amounted to £6,123,177.†

Among other consequences, then, of a general dimi-nution of the value of the precious metals, we may lay our account with a great augmentation of poor rates.

I have already stated, that although a reduction of the interest of money is not a consequence which the

* Porter's Progress of the Nation, p. 86.
† Ib.

increased production of gold is calculated directly to produce—interest depending not on the amount of money in circulation, but on the amount of capital seeking investment—yet during the progress of the change, and while money continues to flow in upon us, a temporary fall in the market rate of interest is to be expected. Whether the fall may be so great as to enable the Chancellor of the Exchequer to effect a reduction of the dividends on 3 per cent. consols—by far the largest portion of our debt, and which government has the option of paying off at par—remains to be seen. If so, the holders of such securities will have an accumulation of evils to contend with—their dividends, reduced in amount as well as diminished in value, will be subject to higher public taxes than they were before, while local rates and burdens will at the same time be proportionally increased.

# LETTER XXVI.

*Probable effects of the gold discoveries on the condition of different classes of society—labourers—capitalists—landlords—tenants—public officers—annuitants—stipendiaries—debtors—creditors, &c.—Objections to reverting to a silver standard—concluding remarks.*

As long as yearly additions continue to be made to the metallic wealth of Europe, from the abundant deposits which have lately been discovered, it is impossible to doubt that a powerful and wholesome stimulus will be given to industry and legitimate enterprise in all the departments of production. "In every kingdom," says Hume, "into which money begins to flow in greater abundance than formerly, every thing takes a new face, labour and industry gain life, the merchant becomes more enterprising, the manufacturer more diligent and skilful, and even the farmer follows his plough with greater alacrity and attention."*

It is during the progress of the consequent change from low to high prices, that the chief benefit of those new sources of wealth which providence has opened up to us will be experienced by the producing classes. When the effect has been fully produced, all things will return to their former state. The artisan who now earns half-a-crown a-day will be quickened into renewed diligence as long as his wages are in process of augmentation. But the increase of money consequent on the diminished cost of the metals will not raise the price of labour only, but the prices of all things. The enhancement of money wages will probably be preceded by the enhancement of the money value of commodities, and after the rise of wages and prices has become general, the labourer will be no better off than before. As prices are now adjusted, his money wages enable him to command a certain amount, whatever it be, of the necessaries and conveniencies of life. In these, and not in the money which he receives, his real remuneration consists. Increase his money wages from half-a-crown

* Hume's Political Discourses, 2d edit. p. 47.

to five shillings, and double at the same time the price
of his food, his clothing, his fuel, and lodging, everything, in short, which he has occasion to purchase, or
wishes to consume, and after the change he will be able
to live no better than at present.  His nominal wages
have advanced, but his real wages have not been increased.  He gets more money, but he acquires no
additional command over the goods which that money
will purchase.

In countries where gold is an imported commodity,
procured, not by direct labour, but in exchange for other
commodities, a rise in the money price of provisions and
products generally may be expected to precede, though
probably by a very short interval, a general enhancement of money wages.  This would appear to have been
the case in England in the sixteenth century, and again
when the second rise of prices occurred after the middle
of the eighteenth century.  And should the effects of
the recent gold discoveries develop themselves in the
same order, our working-classes, unlike the labourers
of the gold producing countries, may in the first instance have to contend with a fall of real wages, that is,
of wages estimated not in money but in commodities.
But this effect will be transient.   The enhanced money

value of commodities, and the great increase of floating capital, will speedily lead to a readjustment; and money wages will rise until the labourer reacquire his former command over the necessaries of life.

Nor will the capitalist ultimately be in a better situation. His profits depend upon the proportion between his outgoings and his returns. Increase the amount of money in general circulation, and his returns will be raised in pecuniary value; but if his outgoings are raised, as ultimately they must be in the same proportion, the *rate* of his profits will not be increased. The *amount* of his profits will be greater, but he will in reality be no richer than before, because the increased amount will purchase no more of the necessaries and luxuries of life than the smaller nominal amount which he now receives. Suppose, for example, that a manufacturer now employs in his business a capital worth £1000, and has a return of £1100, his profits are 10 per cent. Again, suppose that in consequence of a general enhancement of prices, his capital comes to be worth £2000, and that his returns, from the same cause, are increased in money value to £2200, his profits will still be 10 per cent.; and £200, after the prices of labour and all commodities have been doubled, and his rates and taxes also doubled, will go no farther in the expenses of living than £100 at present. Before the readjustment takes place he will be a gainer; but after the full effect upon prices has been produced, all things will return to their present relative position, and the capitalist will have nothing farther to expect from the reduction in the value of money.

As regards the agricultural interest, the change will affect landlords and tenants variously. By the proprietor who cultivates his own lands an improvement will be instantly experienced. He stands in a position, in this respect, similar to that of the manufacturer. The money value of his corn, his cattle, and other produce, will be enhanced, but concurrently there will be a proportional rise in the money value of the capital employed in cultivation. Rent and profits will increase in money value, but after the change has been fully effected, the increased amount will go no farther than the present amount in the purchase of commodities and the expense of living.

To the tenant who has just entered upon a lease, for suppose twenty-one years, at a fixed money rent adjusted with reference to existing prices, the change will bring twenty-one years of increasing wealth and prosperity.

To the landlord, who must wait until the expiration of this term for an increase of rent, and who must in the interval pay double for every thing he consumes, with increased rates and taxes, and interest and jointures not diminished, the change will bring twenty-one years of hardship and privation. After the lapse of this period neither party will be a gainer—the rent will be proportioned to the new scale of prices—and that rent, so augmented, will go no farther than the landlord's present income in furnishing him with the necessaries and luxuries of life.

In the case of the clergy, whose incomes rise and fall with the average money price of corn, the change will be little felt. Not so with naval and military officers, judges, civil functionaries, and all who have fixed pecuniary incomes. In their case, a general reduction of the value of money will diminish their means of living to a corresponding extent, and the hardship will continue until stipends and pensions are raised in proportion to the general advance of prices.

But the classes whom this alteration of prices will most sensibly affect are the debtor and creditor classes of the community. The landlord whose estate is charged with dower or with provisions to younger children, or a reserved rent in perpetuity, will find his burdens materially lightened; for although the pecuniary amount of these burdens will not be diminished, his rents, his returns, his means of meeting these payments, will be greatly increased. The mortgager will benefit to a corresponding extent, and for the same reason, while the creditor, the mortgagee, will be the sufferer. He has lent, we shall suppose, £1000 upon the security of a land estate, to bear interest at 4 per cent. Under this covenant he will still receive £40 a-year as before; but that sum, if reduced one-half in purchasing power, will command, in all time to come, only one-half the quantity of commodities which it now does. In a word, during the progress of the change, the producing classes will be the gainers, and consumers will be the losers. The former will benefit temporarily—the latter, at least those of them who live upon fixed incomes, will suffer in perpetuity. Debtors will get richer, creditors will get poorer. Production, in all the departments of industry, agricultural and manufacturing, will be powerfully excited and stimulated. Rents, wages, and profits, will be elevated simultaneously. Money will everywhere abound, and the country will rapidly advance in material prosperity. The creation and accumulation of capital—meaning by capital not gold and silver, but materials, provisions, and tools, permanent improvements on land, the construction of docks, railways, canals, bridges, ships, and useful machines, improved means of living, and increased production of commodities in all the departments of industry—will be the ultimate consequence of the gold discoveries; and in this, rather than in the direct and immediate effects, the true value of these discoveries will be found to consist.

But while there is no denying that these beneficial consequences will result from the great monetary changes upon which we seem now about to enter, let it not be forgotten, that during the progressive development of these changes there will be a fearful breaking up of all the existing relations of property. Before the revolution is accomplished, much suffering must be endured by large classes of the community. "If money be flowing in," says Harris, "some branches of trade will be enlivened, and in reality great numbers of individuals will grow richer; as what they pay in taxes, rents, and for material products, will be less, or of less value than before, till you come to the lowest class, who, though their wages are raised, will yet find little or no advantage by this torrent of money. On the other hand, the government will grow weaker, the nobility, and in general all who live upon estates and established stipends, will become poorer, till by an increase of taxes, advancement of rents, &c., things can be re-established. But before this can be accomplished, many and great alterations will naturally happen. The government being thus weakened and distressed, disorders will inevitably arise, as peace and good order cannot be preserved unless the strength of the government bears a due proportion to that of the governed. The nobility must change their fashion of life, and abate of their ancient splendour. New debts will be contracted, increased lands mortgaged, and before the ancient owners have a right understanding of the cause of their distresses, many must part with their estates, and give place to new comers. And this is a natural consequence of a sudden flux of money; the enriching of one part of the community at the expense of the other; a change of manners among all ranks, some perhaps for the better and some for the worse; until this tide having spent itself, things are again resettled, though perhaps in quite a new form."*

* Harris on Money and Coins, Part I. pp. 84, 85.

I quote this passage to you because it appears to me to convey in the main a correct though a somewhat over-coloured picture of what occurred in the reign of Elizabeth and her two immediate successors, and of what took place more than twenty years after Harris's book was written, when a second marked depreciation of the precious metals occurred towards the conclusion of the American war.

But you say, Why not put an end to all doubts and anxiety on this fearfully important subject, and obviate all future risks and difficulties at once, by making silver the sole standard of our money, as it was from the Conquest down to the reign of George the First? Why not do it now, and before any change has taken place in the money price of labour and commodities, or in the relative value of gold and silver? These questions, like many others which have reference to practical legislation, are less easily answered than abstract questions in economical science. Political economy affords some, and those perhaps the most important, but it does not afford all the elements required for their solution. The question of an immediate change of the standard of money involves not considerations of expediency alone, but the far higher considerations of equity and good faith. The legislature has now the power to a great extent, simply by letting things alone, without violating any principle of justice, or trenching upon any law of God or man, to free the overburdened industry and resources of England from the incubus by which they have been so long and so grievously oppressed. Would parliament be justified, then, in stepping in to prevent things from taking that course which nature and providence appear to have beneficently determined they should take? or, assuming that all questions in connexion with our public and national burdens are to be resolved by an appeal to expediency alone, would it be just to oblige private individuals who have contracted pecuniary engagements under stipulations adjusted with reference to one standard of money, to liquidate and fulfil their obligations according to another standard? The man who has undertaken to pay his creditor £100 sterling has in law and in fact engaged to deliver to him 100 sovereigns, or 25⅔ ounces of standard gold. Providence, in the meantime, has furnished the debtor unexpectedly with cheaper and more abundant means of fulfilling this engagement. Is he to be deprived by arbitrary legislation of the benefit of those means? Is parliament to interfere, and to tell him, that because *other* classes of the community may suffer from the increased abundance or more easy acquisition of gold, a burden must be laid upon his shoulders which he never undertook to bear—in other words, that he must now deliver to his creditor not 25⅔ ounces of standard gold, but, because it suits his creditor better, 400 ounces of standard silver?

The question of a change of the standard, I repeat, embraces considerations of justice and equity, as well as considerations of policy and expediency. The economist, therefore, must content himself with pointing out the consequences which are likely to result from adopting a new standard on the one hand, or of adhering to the present standard on the other; and having done so, he ought to hand over the question to the politician or practical statesman. With Mr Senior, I am of opinion that " the business of a political economist is neither to recommend nor to dissuade, but to state general principles which it is fatal to neglect, but neither advisable nor perhaps practicable to use as the sole or even the principal guides in the actual conduct of affairs."*    " In the meantime," adds Mr Senior,—and with the follow-

---

* Article, "Political Economy," in Encyclop. Metropolitana, by N. W. Senior, Esq.

ing weighty sentences, I shall conclude this series of letters,—" In the meantime, the duty of each individual writer is clear. Employed as he is upon a science, in which error, or even ignorance, may be productive of such intense and such extensive mischief, he is bound, like a juryman, to give deliverance true according to the evidence, and to allow neither sympathy with indigence, nor disgust at profusion or at avarice—neither reverence for existing institutions, nor detestation of existing abuses—neither love of popularity, nor of paradox, nor of system, to deter him from stating what he believes to be the facts, or from drawing from those facts what appear to him to be the legitimate conclusions. To decide in each case how far these conclusions are to be acted upon belongs to the art of government, an art to which political economy is only one of many subservient sciences; which involves the consideration of motives of which the desire for wealth is only one among many, and aims at objects to which the possession of wealth is only a subordinate means."

# NOTE.

# NOTE.

---

THE following Extracts are from important notices which appeared
in the *Times* of 18th and 24th November 1852, while the foregoing
sheets were passing through the press :—

" Meroo Creek, on the Turon, the spot on which Dr Kerr's
hundredweight nugget of gold was found in 1851, has lately
again become celebrated for the largeness of its nuggets, few
and far between as they appear to be. Two men found there
a waterworn lump weighing 157 ounces, and they found, also,
a smaller lump of 71 ounces. Accounts equally cheering come
from other localities. At the Dirthole and Tamboora Creek
'£14 worth of gold per man' is considered a fair weekly yield,
while a lucky fellow will earn from £28 to £38, and no man is
thought to be doing well who earns less than £1 per day. In
another locality, the 'Hanging Rock,' the miners average 16½
ounces per week, and in some instances a man made from six
to nine ounces per day. Of course these are exceptional cases ;
some men made little or nothing, and an instance is quoted of
three men who took out eight ounces in less than ten minutes.
The real treasures of the Hanging Rock districts are, however,

still hidden.  It is a deep 'location,' and the miners have hitherto
only been surfacing.  Mr Hargreaves, the first discoverer of the
Australian gold, is of opinion that the colonies have not only a
western and southern, but also a northern gold-field, including
the head of the Peel, the whole of the Hanging Rock district,
the Swamp Oak Creek, and the head of the Macdonald River,
a semicircular tract of country extending above seventy miles,
and auriferous throughout.  The practical results obtained at the
Hanging Rock diggings go far to prove the truth of Mr Hargreaves' hypothesis.  The northern fields, including the Hanging
Rock, cannot, however, be considered as fairly tested.  The
auriferous tract of country is large and the diggers are few;
they have hitherto roamed about without working really and
seriously in any one locality.  The Government Commissioner
Durbin, who has been watching the proceedings at Hanging
Rock, fully concurs with Mr Hargreaves' opinion, and in his
report to the Colonial Office he expresses his conviction that rich
diggings will eventually be opened over the Australian Agricultural Company's Grant.  He has come to that conclusion from
observing the geological structure of that district, with its schis-
tose slate intersected by veins of quartz.  As for the Hanging
Rock district, there are about 400 miners there, all surfacing, as
we said before, and neglecting the treasures of the deep.  But
they are all doing well, and the comparatively small number of
persons who know of the existence of these diggings consider
them more valuable than even those of Mount Alexander and
Bendigo.

" Events rush on at an alarming speed in the gold colonies.
Where will it end?  The last mail, about a fortnight since,
brought the news of the Bendigo diggings, with circumstantial

accounts of their enormous yield and increasing population. The information we have to-day tells us of the Hanging Rock treasures and the northern gold-fields, while further news of the Agricultural Grant diggings are looming in the distance. Not a word about the Bendigo diggings. Have they been swamped by the rain; or were they, after all, a fair delusion? No such thing. Bendigo is as rich as ever; but it has lost the charm of novelty. But that it is yielding, and enormously, is proved by a small paragraph in the *Launceston Examiner*, in which it is said that Mr Bell, watchmaker, purchased 1124 oz. 7 dwts. of gold, the product of the labour of four men, in six weeks, at the Bendigo diggings. This makes, in longer reckoning and round numbers, rather more than £140 a-week for each man; but these, it appears, are stale marvels, and our Australian countrymen think it hardly worth their while to mention them, rolling as they are in gold.

. . . . . . . . . .

" In a former account we mentioned that the escort from Mount Alexander which arrived at Melbourne on the 12th June brought 50,238 ounces of gold. We now learn that this was not the whole amount then in hand at Mount Alexander, but that 20,000 ounces remained at that time in the hands of the Commissioner, who could not send them from want of the means of transport. Mount Alexander, it is stated, has an average yield of 24,284 ounces per week. However large this total may appear, it is little if compared to the number of the miners in that locality which our last accounts quoted at 60,000; and considering the high price of the provisions (flour cost at Melbourne £22 per ton, and carriage to Mount Alexander was £60), it must be confessed that some of these gold-seekers and gold-senders are in an un-enviable position. A rush from Mount Alexander is expected upon Bendigo and the newest diggings at Hanging Rock, and this rush is likely to do much good to either locality. The last escorts from other diggings which are mentioned in the Sydney circulars of the 10th of July brought a very small amount— about £4800 worth of gold from Braidwood, Sofala, Bathurst, Ophir, Goulburn, and Tamworth. But it is stated that the weather has been so unfavourable, and travelling so nearly impossible, that it is a matter of surprise how a single ounce has come down.

" A very interesting document has been published in the shape of a report by Mr Harding, the Chief Gold Commissioner, containing statements of the progress or decline of the various goldfields. From this source we learn that from May to August 1851, there were from 600 to 800 persons at work at Ophir, each earning 20s. per day, but, from rain and other causes the number is now reduced to about 100. Mr Harding thinks, however, that a very extensive and rich gold field is untouched at Ophir, and that nothing but a population is required to find gold in abundance. At the Turon in October last, there were about 4000 diggers employed, but these are now reduced to 1500, solely because it became a fashion to go to Mount Alexander, and in no way from the want of a remunerative gold field at the Turon. At the Meroo there are about 800 persons at work, and there is room for as many thousands. The river is very rich, and has been very little worked. At Tambouroura there are about 800 persons, all doing well. Tenna Creek has about 100 miners, and yet this place and Mulgunnia Creek, Mr Harding says, are as rich as any other places yet discovered. 100 persons are at Arluen Valley and 200 at Mungarlow River, and in either place there is room for thousands. The revenue derived from the gold mines for licenses and escort-fees, from the 1st of November

1851 to the 31st of May 1852, amounted to £46,545. The
expenditure was £20,199, leaving a surplus of £26,346. The
quantity of gold exported from Sydney, since the 31st of October
1851, to the 15th of June 1852, amounted to 384,116 oz., valued
at £1,248,377 ; and the total of the gold exported up to the 10th of
July represented a value of £1,620,600."—*Times*, 18*th Nov.* 1852.

" The accounts from the Australian gold fields up to the end
of August last contain news of the most exciting nature. All
that could have been expected during the prevalence of the win-
try rains of June, July, and August, was not too great a decrease
in the yield of gold. We were prepared for a decrease, and, indeed, the announcement of this most natural contingency had
reached this country by means of Australian papers and letters,
recounting the depopulation of the mines throughout the month
of June, and the comparatively small yields obtained by the diggers that could not leave the mines. But within a few weeks the
tables were turned ; the floods, which for the time spoilt some
' diggings,' opened the hidden wealth of others ; new gold-fields
were found, and astounding results obtained. Mount Alexander
sent down 22,402 ounces to Geelong in the last week of July, and
in that week Ballarat sent 1572 ounces. On the 3d of August
the Mount Alexander escort had 18,145 ounces ; and on Monday
and Thursday following the amounts transmitted were 71,145 and
18,174 ounces, making a total of 107,384 ounces in the first seven
days of August, and from one locality ! The amount transmitted
from Ballarat in the same space of time was 2066 ounces, and
Dight's escort brought 34,676 ounces, so that a grand total of
144,207, representing about £432,621, were received within seven
days at Geelong. This enormous sum does not, however, repre-

sent the whole of the weekly yield of the Victoria mines, for large quantities of gold had accumulated at the diggings; the roads were bad, and the means of conveyance limited. The total amount transmitted up to the 14th of August was 53,998 ounces from Ballarat, Mount Alexander, and by Dight's escort. On the 19th of August Ballarat sent to Melbourne 1000 ounces, and 3848 to Geelong, while 1000 ounces were left behind for want of means of conveyance. On the 21st of August 36,985 ounces came from Ballarat and by Dight's. On the 25th of August Ballarat sent 4167, and Mount Alexander sent 842 ounces. At that date a large quantity of gold was left behind at Ballarat; and the next escort, if it could get horses, was expected to bring down above 10,000 ounces. On a rough calculation, which is rather under than over the mark, the Victoria diggings yielded in the month of August about 246,000 ounces of gold—and this, too, in the rainy season, and with not a very considerable increase of their mining population. What the figures will amount to when the population at the fields is doubled—and doubled it soon will be, in the presence of such exciting news—it is difficult to foretell; but, judging from the result already obtained, the quantities of gold which will be dug out are perfectly bewildering.

" Every mail brings fresh marvels. In addition to the enormous yields of the mines whose names are already familiar to the British public, new spots, teeming with the precious metal, are continually being discovered; and every file of papers introduces us to some new and until then never heard of locality. Thus, for instance, there are several spots in the vicinity of Forest Creek which have acquired a sudden and brilliant fame. One place, 'a flat,' between Adelaide Gully and Wattletree Flat, on the road leading from Forest Creek to Fryer's Creek, has obtained colonial celebrity by a party of four Adelaide men, who had gone there 'prospecting,' turning up 150 lb. weight of pure gold in one morning between breakfast and dinner. That is to say, £6000 worth of sterling money obtained in one hole in the course of one morning. Another hole has, of course, been sunk immediately, closely adjoining 'the claim' of these lucky fellows, and here, too, the daily yield averaged from six to nine pounds weight of gold. In the whole line of the gullies and flats in that vicinity the diggers have been eminently successful. Many in the neighbourhood have taken 9, 12, and 20 pounds weight in 'pockets,' but, of course, the 150 pounds of gold we quoted above stands as yet unparalleled in the history of gold-finding. It is high time to revise the *Arabian Nights' Entertainments*. Pillars of gold and baskets filled with precious stones cannot dazzle the imagination of the rising generation, when the wildest flights of romance are left behind by commonplace matter of fact reality. Seven tons of gold were lying idle at Adelaide Gully for want of horses to take them to Melbourne, and more was fast accumulating. At New Bendigo Flat, Forest Creek, one 'party' took 12 lb. weight from one hole, and four Germans gained 21 lb. of gold in one week. At Donkey Gully, in the upper part of Forest Creek, 100 ounces were taken out by a party in one week, and many other diggers in that vicinity are digging the old deserted holes, and doing 'very well.'

"The Bendigo diggings, which we mentioned in a late report, have been spoiled by the floods, at least for the time being. Snow, seven feet deep, has fallen, which is quite a rarity in Australia, and the snow which covers the hills of Bendigo has given the finishing touch to that gold-field. The diggers have left it, but not for Geelong or Melbourne, but for Mount Korong and

Mount Cole, two new localities, of which no particulars have at
present reached us, but which are likely to play a conspicuous
part in the 'Gold Circulars' of next year.  But there are accounts,
and great news too, of the last new diggings at Eureka, near
Ballarat, which have turned out one of the largest nuggets yet
found in Victoria.  The nugget weighs, freed from all impurities,
102 oz., and resembles in shape a cramped hand.  It was found
in Bunigong Gully, Eureka, by a Mr Mould, who was offered
£330 for it.  The Eureka diggings are deep; the miners make
circular holes fifty feet down; the yield is steady, and occasionally there are large 'finds.'  The gold is very beautiful and pure,
but more ragged than that of Ballarat, and evidently not so much
water-washed.  Not one gully had failed at the end of August.
The diggers were established in commodious tents and huts;
stores had sprung up, and it was thought 'a work of supererero-
gation' to repeat continually instances of gain.  Perhaps there
are two opinions on that point.  But the satisfactory result of
three letters from Eureka is that all are doing well, and that they
only want more 'hands' to do better still.  .  .  .  .

"The papers before us contain a very interesting document,
a price current of labour, published by a Mr Fitchett, of the Victoria Registry Office.  Of course the prices are *bonâ fide* ones,
because Mr Fitchett is prepared to engage servants at the amount
he mentions.  Married couples, as house servants for country
hotels, &c., can have engagements at £65 to £70 per annum,
with rations; shepherds, £38; hutkeepers, £30; bullock-drivers,
£50, or by the week, £1, 10s., and on the roads from £3 to £4;
farm-servants, £50 per annum, and £1, 10s. by the week; bush-
carpenters, £2 per week; cooks for inns, £1, 10s. to £2 per week;
general servants £40 per annum, all including rations.  Maid

servants can have engagements at £24 to £30, housemaids at £23, nursemaids £18, cooks and laundresses £24, including rations. This was the state of the labour market *after* the arrival of several emigrant vessels; and though it may experience a temporary decline in the course of the next twelvemonth, prices are expected to 'hold,' and a rise is even expected at no distant period.

" The prices of provisions went, to adopt the expression of a Sydney correspondent, ' up and down' like a barometer. On the 11th of August, flour sold at Forest Creek at £12 per bag; sugar at 1s. 6d. per lb.; salt was 2s.; tea, 4s.; cheese, 3s. 6d.; ham and salt pork, 4s.; beef, 8d. per lb.; biscuits, 2s. 6d. per lb. About the same time the quotations in the Melbourne market were—flour (at the mills, that is to say *minus* carriage), £25; wheat, 8s.; and oats, 7s. 6d. Good cattle sold at 12s. per cwt.; sheep, 11s. The price of butcher-meat was rising generally, but flour and bread were not expected to rise higher, since the markets were more freely supplied. The Launceston and Hobart Town markets remained almost unchanged; wheat at 9s., and first flour at £24; barley, 5s.; potatoes, £4. At Hobart Town there was an advance of 1s. generally on the Launceston prices.

" £200,000 in specie was imported from England into Victoria in the first week of August, by the Dalhousie, Mermaid, and the steamer Chusan."—*Times*, 24*th Nov.* 1852.

THE END.